Brown v. Board of Education

School at Anthoston, Henderson County, Kentucky.

Brown v. Board of Education

A FIGHT FOR SIMPLE JUSTICE

SUSAN GOLDMAN RUBIN

HOLIDAY HOUSE / NEW YORK

Book design by Trish Parcell Watts
HOLIDAY HOUSE is registered in the U.S. Patent and Trademark Office.
Printed and Bound in June 2016 at Toppan Leefung, DongGuan City, China.
www.holidayhouse.com
First Edition
1 3 5 7 9 10 8 6 4 2
Library of Congress Cataloging-in-Publication Data

Names: Rubin, Susan Goldman, author.
Title: Brown v. Board of Education : a fight for simple justice / Susan
Goldman Rubin.
Description: New York : Holiday House, 2016.
Identifiers: LCCN 2016004631 | ISBN 9780823436460 (hardcover)
Subjects: LCSH: Brown, Oliver, 1918-1961—Trials, litigation, etc.—Juvenile
literature. | Topeka (Kan.). Board of Education—Trials, litigation,
etc.—Juvenile literature. | Segregation in education—Law and
legislation—United States—Juvenile literature. | African
Americans—Civil rights—Juvenile literature.
Classification: LCC KF228.B76 R83 2016 | DDC 344.73/0798—dc23 LC record available at
http://lccn.loc.gov/2016004631

For Linda Brown Smith Thompson, Cheryl Brown Henderson,
John Watson, Jr., Joan Johns Cobb, Barbara Johns Powell, Carrie Stokes,
John Arthur Stokes, Harry Briggs, Jr., Spottswood Thomas Bolling, Jr.,
Shirley Barbara Beulah Stamps, Ethel Louise Belton Brown,
and the hundreds of other people who were part of
Brown v. Board of Education.

TABLE OF CONTENTS

Brown v. Board of Education

A FIGHT FOR SIMPLE JUSTICE

INTRODUCTION:
WHAT IS SEGREGATION?

WHEN John Stokes and his twin sister, Carrie, started school in Farmville, Virginia, in 1940, they were nine years old. They had to wait till they were big enough to walk the four and a half miles along a busy highway to reach the school for black children. There were no buses for black children. The twins' protective older brothers, Howard and Leslie, who went to the black high school, next to the elementary school, walked with John and Carrie.

"The trip wasn't so bad on nice days," recalled John, "but when it was hot or rainy, we were miserable. The worst part was when a bus carrying white kids to school passed us. Sometimes they would spit at us and call us names."

Walking home at night was much worse. White drivers sometimes stopped and attacked blacks. One day when John was twelve he attended a Boy Scout meeting led by the principal of his school. John's parents had told him to come straight home to the farm after the meeting so he could walk while it was still daylight. But John disobeyed and "slipped into downtown Farmville to go to the movies with some other kids." In those days in the South, movie theaters were

Opposite: A picture titled "How about a decent school for me?" from the NAACP collection of photographs of schools and activities to end segregation. 1940–1960

1

A classroom heated by a potbellied stove in the main building of Robert R. Moton High School, Farmville, Virginia. 1952

segregated, just like public schools. Farmville had one theater for white people only, and another for both races, but black people entered separately and had to sit in the balcony. After the show, John raced home.

"I was so terrified that night," he recalled. "During this time," wrote John, it was not unusual "for colored boys and girls to be taunted, hurt and even killed, especially if they were caught alone at night." Whenever a car approached, he hid. His mother and father had warned him to "take cover in ditches and gullies, behind bushes and trees" if he walked after dark.

Finally, he reached his farm. "I pray to God and thank him that I made it home safe," he said at the time.

Blacks in the Jim Crow era faced constant danger. "Jim Crow was a derogatory term for a black person...that caused us to be treated as second-class citizens," explained John. The term sprang from a songbook published in Ithaca, New York, in 1839. The book ridiculed a minstrel show character named Jim Crow. By the 1890s the expression was used to describe customs and laws that segregated people on the basis of the color of their skin.

Blacks were known then as "coloreds" or "Negroes." In the South, blacks could not use the same public bathrooms or drinking fountains as whites. It was against the law for blacks to talk with whites on the streets. Blacks couldn't try on clothes and shoes in department stores. At first, streetcars, buses and trains were segregated, then restaurants, boarding houses, hotels, telephone booths, baseball parks and playgrounds all followed suit. In South Carolina, courts even had special Bibles for swearing in black people as witnesses. In Topeka, Kansas, the swimming pool at Gage Park was off-limits to blacks except during a "gala picnic" one day a year. Restaurants downtown had a sign in the window reading NEGROES AND MEXICANS SERVED IN SACKS ONLY. This meant they could order food but could not eat it on the premises. Laws prevented blacks from voting or made it nearly impossible for them to register to vote.

There were also unspoken rules. If a white person accused a black person of

"Colored waiting room" at the bus station in Durham, North Carolina

A one-teacher Negro school in Veazy, Greene County, Georgia. 1941

not "knowing his or her place," the punishment could be "jail time, a beating, or worse." Worse meant a lynching. Lynchings occurred when mobs of whites took the law into their own hands and tortured and murdered black boys and men suspected of committing what white people considered crimes. This could be making eye contact with a white woman, speaking to her or bumping up against her. These constant threats of violence intimidated blacks, and allowed whites to retain power.

In the South, black children were almost never allowed to attend the same school as white children. However, school segregation existed in the North, too. Local governments in Illinois, Ohio, Pennsylvania and New Jersey enforced segregation in public schools even though these states had laws that prohibited the practice.

As early as 1849 in Boston, Massachusetts, a five-year-old girl named Sarah Roberts attended a grammar school for blacks. The school was run-down and badly neglected. Her father, Benjamin F. Roberts, tried to enroll her in one of the better elementary schools for whites near their home. When the Massachusetts school board turned him down, he took his case to court. His lawyer, renowned politician and abolitionist Charles Sumner, argued that a segregated school could never be the equal of a white school. Children should not be separated because of their skin color. However, the judge ruled that segregation was legal.

The decision in the Roberts case then supported the later United States Supreme Court ruling in *Plessy v. Ferguson*. This case came about in 1892 when a light-skinned black man, Homer Adolph Plessy, boarded a train in New Orleans and dared to sit in a car reserved for whites. The conductor asked him to move into the car for "colored passengers." Plessy refused. A detective standing nearby arrested him and sent him to jail. Plessy hired a lawyer, and the case went to trial in New Orleans. Plessy argued that the segregation law in Louisiana violated the Fourteenth Amendment, which guaranteed equal rights to all citizens of the United States. But the judge ruled against him, and the case was appealed in the Louisiana Supreme Court. From there,

Plessy took his case to the Supreme Court of the United States.

At last, in 1896, the Court handed down its opinion: Segregation in America was legal. Racially separate facilities such as schools did not violate the Constitution as long as they were equal. *Plessy v. Ferguson* established "separate but equal" as the law of the land.

By 1912, President Woodrow Wilson had segregated government offices in Washington, D.C., as well. Curtains separated the desks of the few black men who held government jobs in Wilson's administration. Cafeteria tables were assigned racially, and the lunchroom in the Library of Congress was segregated during Wilson's presidency. Many blacks in government jobs were fired or demoted.

In 1908, Thoroughgood Marshall was born in Baltimore, Maryland. At age six he shortened his name to Thurgood. "It was too damn long," he later explained, "so I cut it." He even had his mother change it on his birth certificate.

Thurgood's paternal grandfather, Thorney Good Marshall, had been a slave who escaped and ended up in Baltimore. His grandfather Isaiah O. B. [Olive Branch] Williams, a political activist, had battled with Baltimore officials about admitting black children to public schools. His father, William Marshall, worked as a sleeping-car porter on the railroad. Although William had dropped out of grammar school, he wanted his sons, Thurgood and Aubrey, to be well educated. Thurgood's mother, Norma, had graduated from teachers college but stayed home to take care of her children.

In 1909, the year after Thurgood was born, the National Association for the Advancement of Colored People (NAACP) was founded to stop the abuse of blacks. Headquarters were located in New York City, and in 1912, a branch opened in Baltimore. "Everybody in my family was mad about segregation," recalled Thurgood.

As a boy he attended a segregated public school. Not every aspect of his life was segregated, however. He lived next door to a white Jewish family that owned a grocery store. He and the owner's son Sammy Hale played together and became best friends. "We used to have fights, fusses, because he would let people call him a kike [an offensive term for a Jew] and wouldn't fight back," recalled Marshall. "If anybody called me a 'Nigger' I fought 'em." His father told him to never let an insult go by without standing up

for himself. "Either win or lose right then and there," he instructed.

When Marshall was fifteen, he worked after school for Mr. Schoen, the Jewish owner of a ladies' dress shop. One day, during the five o'clock rush hour, Marshall set out to deliver five hatboxes. He boarded the crowded trolley and accidentally brushed past a white woman. A man grabbed him by the collar and yanked him off the trolley. He called Marshall a derogatory name and yelled, "Don't you push in front of white people!" Marshall dropped the boxes and punched the man. A crowd gathered. A policeman ran over and arrested Marshall. His employer hurried down to the station and told the police that the white man had started the fight. "So they took his word and let me go," recalled Marshall. He apologized for destroying the expensive hats. Mr. Schoen said, "It was worth it if you're right. Did they really call you a nigger?"

"Yes, sir," said Marshall.

Mr. Schoen put his arm around Marshall and told him he had done the right thing.

Marshall attended an all-black high school known as Colored High. The school had no library, cafeteria or gym

Thurgood Marshall at age sixteen in his high school graduation picture

His father attended courtroom trials in his time off and observed the tactics of lawyers, so he made his sons back up their points the way lawyers did. "I got the idea of being a lawyer from my dad," said Marshall.

After graduating from high school at age sixteen, Marshall applied to Lincoln University, a top school in Oxford, Pennsylvania, for black men. A question on the application asked, "What do you plan as your life's work?"

"Lawyer," wrote Marshall.

To earn tuition he worked as a dining-car waiter on the B&O Railroad, then entered college in 1925 when he was seventeen. At Lincoln, he became friends with Langston Hughes, an older student who was already a well-known poet. They discussed Jim Crow practices, which heightened Marshall's awareness of injustice.

After he graduated in 1930, Marshall worked as a waiter in an exclusive club for whites to earn money for law school. He wound up commuting from Baltimore to Howard University Law School in Washington, D.C. Howard was considered second-rate, a "Dummies' Retreat" for black law students. But Dean Charles Hamilton Houston had taken over in

and was so overcrowded that students attended half-day sessions. Marshall acted up in class. One time, as punishment for a prank, the principal sent him down to the basement with the United States Constitution and said he had to memorize it before he could leave. "Before I left that school," recalled Marshall, "I knew the whole thing by heart."

At home, over dinner, he, his father and his brother loudly debated race problems, politics, even the weather. "We'd argue about everything," said Marshall.

Young men pledging the Alpha Phi Alpha fraternity, including Thurgood Marshall (second row, second from the right), during Marshall's freshman year at Lincoln University. 1926

1929 and transformed Howard into a fully accredited law school, turning out brilliant black lawyers. Houston, who had graduated from Amherst College and Harvard Law School, became Marshall's role model and mentor. "He was training lawyers to go out and go in the courts and fight and die for their people," recalled Marshall. "He would tell us, 'Men, you've got to be social engineers. We've got to turn this whole thing around. And the black man has got to do it.'"

During his final year, Marshall helped Houston with a case for the National Association for the Advancement of Colored People (NAACP). "We began to work out this attack on the segregated school system," he said.

By the time Marshall graduated he realized, "The lawyer was there to bear the brunt of getting rid of segregation.... That was our purpose in life."

1. CHALLENGING THE LAW

ON April 4, 1950, hundreds of people lined up outside the United States Supreme Court. Everyone wanted to hear Thurgood Marshall argue a case. Marshall was head lawyer of the Legal Defense and Educational Fund (LDF), a branch of the NAACP. Inside the majestic courthouse, he stood before the nine justices. In an emotional speech, he maintained that his client, Herman Marion Sweatt, a postman and World War II veteran, had a right to attend the University of Texas Law School. Texas officials had refused to admit Sweatt because of his race. They claimed that a separate Jim Crow law school for black students would be equally good. Hurriedly, they had built a school just for Sweatt in the basement of a building in Austin. It did not even have a library.

Marshall argued that segregation was wrong even if the state could build separate and equal schools for blacks. "We are convinced that it is impossible to have equality in a segregated system," he said.

Daniel Black, the Attorney General of Texas, responded by telling the justices that his state wanted to take care of the matter by itself. If Sweatt was admitted

Portrait of Thurgood Marshall created between 1935 and 1940

Marshall called Sweatt with the good news. "We won the big one," he said.

With this triumph, Marshall became a celebrity. He soon became the unofficial spokesperson for blacks in America. *Collier's*, a popular magazine, dubbed him "Our Greatest Civil Liberties Lawyer." The article described him as a "tall, burly, gregarious man, light-skinned and light-hearted." But his wife, Vivian Burey, nicknamed Buster, expressed con-

Mrs. and Mrs. Herman Sweatt standing in front of the Supreme Court Building. 1950

to law school, Black argued, then blacks would have to be admitted to swimming pools, grammar schools and hospitals!

On June 5, the Supreme Court handed down a unanimous decision in favor of Sweatt. The justices agreed that the study of law required an exchange of ideas and views that could not happen in a separate school for blacks. For the first time, a graduate level white school would have to admit a black student even though prior rulings had supported the "separate but equal" laws.

cern for her husband in the article. She said that Marshall, age forty-two, worked constantly, and that it was affecting his health. She said, "It's a discouraging job he's set [for] himself."

Marshall announced that his goal was to "wipe out . . . all phases of segregation in education from professional school to kindergarten." He began holding weekend conferences in his office with NAACP lawyers from across the country. They discussed strategies to get the courts to rule that segregation was unconstitutional.

Robert L. Carter, a black lawyer who was Marshall's chief assistant, brought up a recent case in California, *Mendez v. Westminster School District*. Sylvia Mendez, a nine-year-old girl of Mexican descent, and her brothers Gonzalo Jr. and Jerome, had tried to enroll in a public school in Westminster. But the school secretary had refused to admit them because of their heritage and dark skin. Instead she sent them to a school for Mexican American students in another district. Their father, Gonzalo Mendez, a naturalized citizen and successful farmer, hired a civil rights lawyer and sued the Westminster school district. The lawyer enlarged the case to include five Latino families and filed a lawsuit against four school districts.

The case went to trial on March 18, 1946. Marshall helped by sending a friend-of-the-court brief to the judge arguing that segregation for any reason was wrong. A year later, Judge Paul McCormick ruled in favor of the Mendez family and the other plaintiffs. He said that segregation in the school fostered "antagonisms in the children" and made the Chicano students feel inferior. The school district appealed the decision, but on April 15, 1947, the Ninth Circuit

Robert L. Carter, NAACP attorney. 1955

Court of Appeals in San Francisco unanimously upheld the ruling.

The success of the Mendez case inspired the LDF lawyers to find convincing evidence that segregation harmed black children. Carter spoke of the recent work of psychologist Kenneth Clark, a professor at City College of New York. Clark and his wife, Mamie, had conducted experiments on black children, using dolls. They showed black dolls and white dolls to the children and asked them to choose the dolls they liked best. The boys and girls almost always preferred the white dolls, saying they were prettier and smarter. Marshall agreed that psychological studies would be an effective weapon for fighting segregation. The lawyers also had to care-

fully pick "school cases," as they called them, that could be won in court. Dozens of complaints and briefs crossed Marshall's desk every day. But he wanted a small number of representative cases from different parts of the country, not just from the Deep South where Jim Crow practices were the worst.

At that time the LDF, known as the Fund, had five school cases from four states and the District of Columbia in trial courts. In 1953, when the lawyers appealed these cases, the Supreme Court combined them for argument and decision. When the second case happened to be moved to the head of the list, by accident all five were filed under that name: *Brown v. Board of Education.*

Sylvia Mendez as a young girl. 1947
Courtesy of the Mendez family

2. LINDA CAROL BROWN

WHEN Linda Carol Brown was about to enter third grade her father walked her over to Sumner Elementary School to enroll her despite the fact that at that time, 1950, all the elementary schools in Topeka, Kansas, were segregated. Linda had been attending Monroe School, which was for black children. Sumner was for white children only.

The Browns thought Linda Carol's commute to school was unsafe. To get the bus to Monroe School, Linda walked six blocks and crossed the Rock Island Railroad switching yard, which was filled with huge locomotives being detached from freight cars. The yard was a deserted maze of tracks. "I was very much afraid for her to have to go up the busy railroad track and cross the streets," said Linda's mother, Leola Brown.

"Many times she had to wait through the cold, the rain and the snow until the bus got there," said her father, Oliver Brown. Linda rode the bus for half an hour. If the bus came on time by eight o'clock, she reached Monroe before it opened and had to stand outside till nine.

Sumner Elementary, however, was just seven blocks from her house. The

Linda and Terry Lynn Brown walking to school through the railroad yards in Topeka, Kansas. January 1954

front steps of the school that morning, she knew her father was tense. Linda stayed with the school secretary while her father went into the principal's office. "I could hear voices and hear [my father's] voice raised as the conversation went on," she said. "Then he immediately came out of the office, took me by the hand and we walked home from the school. I remember his grip was much firmer going home. I could tell something was bothering him. I just couldn't understand what was happening, because I was so sure that I was going to get to go to school with Mona, Guinevere, Wanda and all of my playmates."

Years later, Linda discovered that the principal had told her father that although he was not opposed to integrated schools, the school board was, and there was nothing he could do about it. Back in 1896, the Supreme Court had ruled that separate facilities for white people and black people were permissible as long as they were judged to be equal.

racially mixed neighborhood, though mostly white, included "Negro" families like the Browns as well as Mexicans and Native Americans. "I had all of these playmates of different nationalities," recalled Linda. "When I found out that I might be able to go to their school I was just thrilled."

As Linda and her father climbed the

"My mom and dad, they did sit me down and try to explain to me, you can't go to school with Wanda, and Guinevere and Mona, because of the color of your skin," recalled Linda. "I really didn't comprehend what they were talking about.... All I knew is that I wanted to go to school with these playmates."

So Linda entered third grade at Monroe. The school was dark brick and older than Sumner, but the teachers were excellent. Many of them had advanced degrees. Linda's black teacher, Mamie Luella Williams, was considered the best in Topeka. "She was a brilliant woman," said Linda, "a staunch, old-time teacher who really made you apply yourself. I respected her a great deal."

Yet Linda had to continue to make that long trip across the busy freight railroad yard every day. Her father, usually a quiet man, felt upset. He worked as a welder in the Santa Fe Railroad repair shops and had become an assistant pastor at a Methodist church near their home. The Browns were a religious family. Linda and her two younger sisters, Cheryl and Terry, said grace before dinner, prayers at bedtime and attended Sunday school every week. "Our friends would get to go to the show on Sunday afternoon and we couldn't," said Linda, "because Dad

Sumner School, second and third grades, Topeka, Kansas. December 17, 1952

Linda Brown (seated in the front row on the right) in her classroom at Monroe School, Topeka, Kansas. March 1953

was a minister and we had to go back to church."

One evening soon after Linda's father had tried to enroll her at Sumner, he took her to a meeting at the Church of God. That night, McKinley Burnett, son of a slave and a member of the local NAACP, led the congregation. He asked Linda to stand on the podium in the front of the room while someone in the audience shouted, "Why should this child be forced to travel so far to school each day?"

Unbeknownst to Linda, the NAACP had approached her father during the summer. They had urged him to participate in a case that would challenge the law and end segregation in Topeka public schools. Burnett and a legal team had been planning the challenge for a couple of years and were looking for suitable families with similar complaints—families that would be willing to attach their children's names to a lawsuit and stand up and fight for school integration.

Many black parents in Topeka objected like Reverend Brown to the unnecessarily long trips their children made to segregated schools. Lucinda Todd, secretary of the Topeka branch of NAACP, had tried to enroll her daughter Nancy in a white elementary school near their house and had failed. Mrs. Todd had sent a letter to the NAACP office in New York saying that the branch was prepared to go to court to test the school segregation law in Kansas. Lena Mae Carper, wife of the man who ran the laundry room at the Kansan Hotel, had protested to John Scott, a Topeka NAACP lawyer. Mrs. Carper complained that her ten-year-old daughter Katherine had to cross two busy streets to catch a school bus that took her to a school twenty-four blocks away. Yet there were two schools for white children a few blocks away from where they lived.

In the fall of 1950, Burnett had gone before the school board and requested an end to segregation. The board said they would not change their position until the law was changed. So the NAACP decided to file a lawsuit.

Burnett asked twelve other parents in Topeka besides Reverend Brown, Mrs. Todd and Mrs. Carper to participate. "At first he didn't want to do it," said Reverend Brown's wife, Leola, because all the other participants were women. "But they prevailed upon him and he finally consented to be one of the plaintiffs.

"He was one of those who would step forward if there was a cause to be brought forth and talked about or acted upon," said Mrs. Brown. Some people who knew him said that he agreed to join the lawsuit because he believed God approved it.

The lawyers listed the plaintiffs' names alphabetically. Darlene Brown [no relation] came first. But the lawyers put Oliver Brown at the top of the list because they thought a man's name would gain more respect. So on February 28, 1951, attorney Charles Bledsoe paid fifteen dollars to file the case with the United States District Court for Kansas. It was called *Brown v. Board of Education of Topeka.*

3. CHILDREN ARE CRAVING LIGHT

ON June 25, 1951, nobody lined up to hear the trial in Topeka, Kansas. There were empty seats inside the third-floor courtroom of the federal building. Many black people in the community opposed the integration of the schools. Black teachers felt threatened because they feared they might lose their jobs. Linda Brown's teacher, Mamie Williams, was heard to say, "Do you think the white people would have me teach their children?"

Yet Thurgood Marshall chose this case out of several school segregation cases. In Topeka, unlike in the Deep South, the school buildings were almost equal physically. The main focus of the trial in Kansas would be the state's policy of segregation. Marshall had been hired as a civil rights lawyer for the NAACP in 1936 for $2,400 a year plus expenses. "We had absolutely no money at all in those days," he recalled. Cases piled into the Legal Defense Fund, established in 1940, and Marshall brought in dedicated young lawyers to work under him on a full-time basis. Since he couldn't handle every major case himself he sent Robert Carter, a brilliant and experienced black lawyer, and Jack Greenberg, a bright young Jewish lawyer who had recently joined the Fund, to Topeka. They worked with John

Top: Sumner School, second grade classroom, Topeka, Kansas. 1950
Bottom: Monroe School, second grade classroom, Topeka, Kansas. March 1949

and Charles Scott, brothers who were the local NAACP lawyers.

Carter and Greenberg arrived in the Jim Crow town and checked into a "colored hotel." It was terribly dirty and shabby. Greenberg pulled the light cord in the bathroom and part of the ceiling fell down. They quickly arranged to stay in the home of one of the members of the Topeka NAACP.

When the trial began, the lawyers presented their case to a panel of three judges.

Lester Goodell, counsel for the Topeka Board of Education, defended school segregation as "simply a question of law." Carter and his team planned to bring in expert witnesses to testify that segregation not only meant unequal facilities, but it wounded children psychologically for life.

Black schoolchildren also suffered because they had to travel great distances to reach segregated schools. John Scott called plaintiff Lena Mae Carper to the stand. She told about her daughter Kath-

The students represented in *Brown et al. v. Board of Education of Topeka*. From left to right: Vicki Henderson, Donald Henderson, Linda Brown, James Emanuel, Nancy Todd, and Katherine Carper. January 1953

erine's long walk to catch the bus. Sometimes, especially in the winter, the bus came fifteen minutes late, and they had to wait in a grocery store and flag the bus down. Yet Randolph, a school for whites, was located near their house.

Then ten-year-old Katherine eagerly took the stand. She played the piano and loved to perform. Scott asked her to describe the condition of the bus when she rode it in the morning.

"Sometimes when I get on the bus it is loaded, and there is no place to sit," she said.

"And are the children sitting on top of each other?" he asked.

"Yes, sir," she answered.

"In your neighborhood, Katherine, do you live in a neighborhood with white children?"

"Yes, sir."

"What schools do they go to?"

"Randolph," she said. The school for whites.

Next, Oliver Brown testified. Linda was not there that morning. Her family wanted to shield her from the case. Nervously, Reverend Brown described Linda's trek to the school bus stop, which involved crossing through the busy Rock Island Railroad switching yard.

Lawyer Charles Bledsoe asked Reverend Brown if Linda would confront such dangerous conditions if she attended Sumner School.

"Not hardly as I know of," he answered.

Bledsoe asked how far away Sumner School was from their house.

"Seven blocks," said Reverend Brown.

Goodell, the opposing lawyer, then cross-examined Brown and referred to a large map of Topeka divided into school zones. He talked about the number of blocks Linda had to walk and asked if Reverend Brown knew that many white children in town had to walk even farther to reach their schools.

Carter objected to the question, and Judge Huxman said, "Objection will be sustained," meaning that he upheld Carter's disapproval.

Reverend Brown left the stand, and seven more plaintiffs followed. Lucinda Todd said, "I couldn't wait to get up there—we'd been fighting for this for so long. And so many in the black community had thought we were a bunch of crackpots."

When the last plaintiff, Silas Fleming, testified, he said he wanted to explain to the judges why he had joined the lawsuit.

Greenberg held his breath. "We didn't

Linda Brown rides to school in Topeka, Kansas. March 1953

know what he [Fleming] was going to say," he wrote. "Sometimes witnesses have a way of giving their lawyers very unpleasant surprises—such as saying they didn't really want to be witnesses or they were testifying against their will."

Fleming began by saying that he had not joined the lawsuit to criticize black teachers who taught his sons, Silas and Duane. "They [the teachers] are supreme, extremely intelligent, and are capable of teaching my kids or white kids or black kids," he said. "But my point was that not

only I and my children are craving light—the entire colored race is craving light, and the only way to reach the light is to start our children together in their infancy and they come up together."

"Fleming inspired us," recalled Greenberg, "and, maybe, the judges."

The next witness was Professor Hugh Speer of the University of Kansas, who trained elementary school teachers. He presented his findings after having inspected the Topeka schools. The buildings for black children were older, but the courses offered were about the same. The important difference was that black children didn't have opportunities to associate with white children. Yet they were living in a society that was 90 percent white. Therefore, concluded Professor Speer, "The Topeka curriculum or any school curriculum cannot be equal under segregation."

One of the strongest witnesses was Louisa Holt, an assistant psychology professor at the University of Kansas. In a preparatory meeting the day before the trial began the experts discussed what points they would make. Holt had said, "I knew what I wanted to stress—that separate but equal is a contradiction in terms."

She testified late in the afternoon. Carter asked her if enforced legal separation adversely affected black children. Holt answered that black children would feel a sense of inferiority, and that would affect their motivation for learning. "In some cases," she said, "it can lead to strong motivation to achieve well....In other cases...the reaction may be the opposite." A student might accept feeling inferior, and any attempt to prove otherwise would be "doomed to failure."

When asked if these difficulties could be corrected at the junior high schools in Topeka that were integrated, Holt said it would be too late. Psychologists knew that the earlier an event occurred in life, the more lasting would be the effects.

At the end of the day, one of the mothers of the black families came up to Holt and introduced her daughters. Holt shook their hands. The woman told her girls, "I want you children to remember this day for the rest of your lives."

Five weeks later, on August 3, 1951, the court handed down its unanimous decision.

"We lost," wrote Greenberg, "but in that loss were the seeds of ultimate victory."

4. STAND TOGETHER

THURGOOD Marshall was looking for more school cases to challenge segregation laws, including some in the Deep South where inequalities were glaring. Before working on *Brown v. Board of Education*, he considered a case in Clarendon County, South Carolina, a rural area. In March 1949, he met with Levi Pearson and other angry black parents. They demanded school buses for their children. White children were driven to their schools on a fleet of thirty buses. Black kids had to find their own transportation.

A year earlier Pearson, a farmer and father of Daisy, James and Eloise, had sued local officials for bus service. Marshall and his team had studied the legal papers and developed the brief. But it turned out that Pearson lived just outside his children's school district, so the judge threw the case out of court.

Pearson refused to give up. The local NAACP lawyer, Harold Boulware, called Marshall and asked him to help file a new lawsuit. Now parents wanted more than buses: They demanded that teachers' salaries, school supplies and buildings be equal to those of the whites. The schools for black children in Clarendon County were wooden shacks. They had no running water or flush toilets

Top: Liberty Hill Colored School, Clarendon County, South Carolina. 1950s
Bottom: Sumerton Graded School (for white children), Clarendon County, South Carolina. 1950

like the white schools, only outhouses. Black children had to get their drinking water out of an open bucket with a dipper. One of their two grade schools didn't even have crayons or desks.

"We ain't asking for anything that belongs to these white folks," explained Reverend J. W. Seals, pastor of St. Mark's in the town of Sumerton and a Clarendon parent. "I just mean to get for that little black boy of mine everything that every other white boy in South Carolina gets."

As Marshall listened to parents and members of the NAACP complain about the bus problem and the appalling schools, he admired their courage. Nevertheless, he worried about taking on a case that attacked segregation in this bigoted plantation country. After further consideration, he decided to risk it. However, he advised against tying the case to one plaintiff. Pearson had lost his lawsuit on a technicality. That could happen much more easily with an individual plaintiff. And whites might bully and threaten a single plaintiff to drop out. Marshall told the NAACP that if they could find twenty plaintiffs willing to fight together for school integration, he and the Fund would take on the lawsuit.

Reverend Joseph Albert DeLaine, a preacher, teacher and parent who lived in Sumerton, led the search. Racism infuriated him. As a boy growing up in the area, he had walked five miles and back to a segregated school. Over the summer, he and his wife, Mattie, a schoolteacher, and Reverend Seals organized meetings to recruit plaintiffs. But blacks feared backlash from whites if they joined, a concern that was well founded. DeLaine lost his job as a teacher. Then the Superintendent of Education offered him a position as principal at the black high school if he would stop leading the fight. DeLaine refused.

In October, DeLaine held a rally. He distributed pamphlets that read, "Parents must stand together for the future good of their children and community." Little by little, black farmers signed up. By November, DeLaine had twenty names. They were listed alphabetically. At the top of the list was Harry Briggs, father of five. From then on, the case was known by his name: *Briggs v. Elliott*. Roderick Elliott, the white owner of a sawmill, was the chairman of School District No. 22, where all the children named in the lawsuit went to school.

Before filing the lawsuit, the NAACP Fund sent lawyer Robert Carter to Clarendon County. Carter met with Harry and Eliza Briggs and the other plaintiffs. He wanted them to understand what they were getting into.

"At that point people were being threatened," recalled Carter. "They had to realize that there was a possibility of them losing jobs, even threats of physical violence." After listening to Carter, only one parent backed out. DeLaine found another plaintiff.

Briggs, a gas station attendant for fourteen years, was targeted immediately. "The white folks got kind of sour," he said. "They asked me to take my name off the petition. My boss, he said did I know what I was doin' and I said, 'I'm doin' it for the benefit of my children.'" Then, the day before Christmas, Briggs's boss gave him a carton of cigarettes and fired him.

Briggs's wife Eliza had been working as a maid at a local motel for six years. Her employer told her to take her name off the lawsuit. Eliza said her name wasn't on it, only her husband's. They told her to tell him to remove his name. She said her husband made up his own mind. A week later, she was fired.

Harry Briggs, Jr., age nine, the oldest child in the family, lost his paper route because of warnings to stay out of the white community. He even lost some

of his friends who were afraid to be seen with him.

Other parents who had signed the petition were put out of work as Carter had feared. DeLaine's wife and nieces lost their jobs as teachers. In January 1950, DeLaine wrote a strong letter, mimeographed it and passed it around town. It read: "Is this the price that free men must pay in a free country for wanting their children trained as capable and respectable American citizens? . . . Shall we suffer endless persecution just because we want our children reared in a wholesome atmosphere?"

As a result, DeLaine received hate mail from the Ku Klux Klan. His superior, African Methodist Episcopal Bishop Frank Madison Reid, ordered him to leave the county for his own safety and take charge of a church thirty-five miles away. Undaunted, DeLaine returned to Sumerton on Saturdays and led meetings that inspired hope. "The black people in the county had had nothing to look forward to until then," said DeLaine's nephew Billie Fleming. "Without the schools there was no way to break out."

On December 20, 1950, Marshall filed the case *Briggs v. Elliott*, and the trial was set for May 1951.

5. LASTING INJURY

AS the NAACP prepared for their next case, they knew they would be in an entirely different environment.

Marshall and Carter left New York to go to the city of Charleston, South Carolina, where *Briggs v. Elliott* was being tried in the federal courthouse. On the train down they discussed the case with their expert witness, Kenneth Clark. Clark, a social scientist, had brought along his equipment: a box of dolls. Two of the dolls were pink and two were brown. Clark and his wife, a psychologist, had bought them at a five-and-ten-cent store in Harlem and had been using them in tests to prove that racism caused black children to lose positive images of themselves at an early age.

Marshall said, "I thought it was a promising way of showing injury to these segregated youngsters. I wanted this kind of evidence on the record." Some of the lawyers on the LDF staff thought it was a joke, however. NAACP lawyer Spottswood Robinson III boarded the train in Richmond, Virginia, to join Marshall and Carter and noticed Clark's dolls. "I know these psychology people are a little strange to begin with," he teased, "but what kind of fellow is this one exactly?"

Dr. Kenneth Clark conducting the "Doll Test" with a young male child. 1947

Upon arriving in Charleston, Marshall began preparing the brief with his legal team. During the week before the trial, they collected information about the segregated schools. Meanwhile, Clark conducted his psychological tests, using the dolls with black schoolchildren in Clarendon County. Marshall worried

about Clark's safety. "It's dangerous over there," he said. "The white fellas are *rough* over there." So he arranged for Eugene Montgomery, executive secretary of the South Carolina NAACP, to drive Clark to Sumerton.

Clark quickly found out why Marshall was worried. At their first stop, the white superintendent of schools for District No. 22 said to Montgomery, "Didn't I tell you I didn't want to see you around here any more in this county? I'd hate to have to get my boys do something to you."

Later, Clark admitted that he was scared to death even though NAACP bodyguards protected him. He tested sixteen black children between the ages of five and nine who had been randomly selected. Ten of the children preferred the white doll. Eleven of the children called the black doll "bad."

Clark also gave a coloring test. He asked a seven-year-old girl with dark-brown skin to color a picture of herself. Out of the twenty-four crayons she chose a flesh-colored pink. When he asked her to draw a little boy the color she liked boys to be she picked up a white crayon. "This doesn't show," she explained to Clark. "So she pressed a little harder…in order to get the white crayon to show."

Her drawings disturbed and pained Clark although they proved his point.

On the morning of May 28, 1951, the doors of the Federal Building in Charleston opened for the trial. Hundreds of black people from all over the eastern part of South Carolina streamed into town. They arrived in jalopies, buses and horse-drawn buggies. "Everyone knew how important an occasion it was," reported Ted Poston of the *New York Post*. People lined up outside the courtroom and along the staircase, hoping to get a seat. "I never did get to sit down in the courtroom," recalled James Gibson, a farmer, "but I never got tired of standing that day. The fact that Judge Waring was up there meant that we were going to get a hearing."

Julius Waties Waring, a native of Charleston, had been a typical Southern bigot in his younger years. But as he grew older and heard testimony from exploited blacks, he changed radically. One particular case came before him that moved him. A white South Carolina farmer had held a young black man in a cabin overnight against his will. Many white farmers did this to temporarily enslave blacks and force them to work without pay for a few days. The practice usually went unchecked. Waring defied Southern racist tradition and sent the farmer to jail for violating the Thirteenth Amendment. In another case, Waring ruled in favor of a black teacher who had sued to win a salary equal to what white teachers received.

In his courtroom, Judge Waring ended segregated seating and included black jurors for the first time. He even appointed a black man as his bailiff, a rarity in America in the 1950s. As a result, the white community snubbed him and his second wife. He received threatening letters. The Ku Klux Klan burned a cross on his lawn and hurled chunks of cement through his front window and against the front door.

Now, as the trial began, Marshall counted on Waring to be sympathetic.

Waring was not the only judge trying the case, however. Any case challenging the constitutionality of state laws had to be heard by a special three-judge District Court. The other two judges were George Bell Timmerman, an advocate of white supremacy, and John J. Parker, a staunch Southerner.

At ten a.m. the trial began.

Robert Figg, the state prosecutor, surprised Marshall. Right away Figg admitted that "inequalities" of schools for black children did exist. He claimed, however, that the defendants intended to make improvements. They asked the court for "a reasonable time" to realize their plans.

Marshall argued that he wanted to prove the unconstitutional nature of segregation in the schools, and to do this his team would show the actual inequalities. He then turned the trial over to Carter.

Carter called Matthew Whitehead to the stand. Whitehead, a professor of education at Howard University, had surveyed the schools for blacks in Clarendon County. He reported his findings:

Manning Elementary Colored School, District No. 9, Clarendon County, South Carolina. Late 1930s

The buildings were made of poor materials, the classrooms had no blackboards or maps, the high school had no auditorium or lunchroom, there was no running water in two of the grade schools, and there were no desks. At Rambay grade school, the students struggled to try to write on long tables full of cracks and holes.

Worst of all were the "earth toilets." At Scott's Branch School, which served 694 students, there were just two "out-of-door" toilets for boys and two for girls. Only the girls' "toilets" had seats. "They were not the type which the State Department of Health of South Carolina describes as privies," said Whitehead.

He concluded that children in the black schools were not getting equal facilities or classroom instruction. When he finally left the stand, he said, "I felt good. It was all down there on the record, and I could see it multiplied throughout the South. And you could see it on the faces of the people in the courtroom—a sort of sigh of relief that it had finally all come out."

Carter's next witness, Ellis O. Knox, was also a professor of education at Howard University. Knox stated that he had inspected school systems in ten other major cities. In his opinion, segregated schools never gave black children educa-

tional opportunities equal to those offered whites.

Then Carter called on Kenneth Clark to testify. Clark described his psychological tests that used dolls and crayons. "I have reached the conclusion," he said, "that discrimination, prejudice and segregation have definitely detrimental effects on the personality development of the Negro child.

"These children in Clarendon County ... have been definitely harmed."

More social psychologists testified and supported the views of Clark, Knox and Whitehead.

Figgs's witness for the Clarendon County School District, E. R. Crow, was director of South Carolina's State Educational Finance Commission. Crow boasted about the state's program to build new schools and predicted that Clarendon County would benefit. Figg asked Crow if it would be wise for students in South Carolina to attend integrated schools. Crow answered that the children would not get along peaceably and predicted that integration would result in violence.

Marshall cross-examined Crow and asked, "How much study have you done on the question of racial tension?"

"If you mean formal study to qualify myself as an expert, I have done none."

Marshall asked him how he drew his conclusion as to what would happen if schools were racially mixed.

Crow answered, "Because of my knowledge of what people say."

"Are you speaking of white people?"

"Mainly."

"How many Negroes do you know?"

"That would be impossible to answer," replied Crow.

On the second day, Carter called his last witness, Helen Trager, an educational consultant from Philadelphia. Her studies showed that black children expected to be spurned and shut out from an early age. "A child who expects to be rejected, who sees his group held in low esteem, is not going to function well," she explained.

Figg argued that these feelings began at home before children went to school.

Trager agreed that home played an important part, but children also learned from what they saw on the playground, the bus and in the whole community. She said, "I think the place, however, where education can take place…is the school."

Then Marshall delivered his concluding remarks. If black children went to inferior schools, they felt inferior. Segregation caused black children "lasting, not temporary, injury."

When court was adjourned, many black people in the room rushed over to Marshall to shake his hand. One older man who had had only two years of schooling told a reporter, "We ain't asking the white folks to give us anything new. We're just asking 'em to give back what they stole from us in the first place."

Three weeks later, the Court handed down the opinion of Judges Parker and Timmerman. They denied the plaintiffs' plea to end segregation in the schools. But they ordered the defendants to "promptly" start improving conditions for black children.

Judge Waring disagreed with the Court's opinion and filed a twenty-page dissent. "Segregation in education can never produce equality," he wrote, "and… is an evil that must be eradicated."

6. STUDENT STRIKE!

WHILE Thurgood Marshall battled school segregation in Clarendon County, a sixteen-year-old girl led a protest in Prince Edward County, Virginia.

Barbara Rose Johns, a junior at Robert R. Moton High School in Farmville, Virginia, was fed up. Her one-story school for blacks had been built in 1939 to serve 180 students. By 1950, Barbara's junior year, the school had 450 kids. Three wooden shacks covered with tar paper had been added in 1948 as temporary relief for overcrowded class-rooms. The shacks leaked and were heated by potbelly stoves. The school board kept promising to make improvements, but nothing happened.

Moton High had no cafeteria or gymnasium, and the auditorium was merely a large room with-out fixed seats. There was no locker room, and boys

Barbara Johns. 1952
Courtesy of the Spelman College Archives

Top: Bathroom sinks at Robert R. Moton High School, Farmville, Virginia
Bottom: Students watching a movie in the auditorium of Robert R. Moton High School, Farmville, Virginia. 1952

Shop for boys at Farmville High School for white students, Prince Edward County, Virginia.

on the football team changed clothes in a classroom. They had to practice during the school day and missed class because they had no buses for extracurricular activities. A few broken-down school buses had been assigned to Moton from the white schools, and there weren't enough.

"The man who drove the bus I took, who was also my history teacher, had to make the fires in the shacks each morning to keep us warm," recalled Barbara.

"Some of us had to sit in our coats—it would bother me a lot."

As a member of Student Council, the chorus and a drama group, Barbara often traveled out of Prince Edward County to better-funded schools in other parts of Virginia. The stark differences offended her. Other students also noticed the disparities.

"Some of the boys in the vocational program visited the shop at the white school and came back telling us how nice their whole school was—and how well equipped," said Barbara. "The comparison made me very angry, and I remember thinking how unfair it was."

One day in the fall of 1950, Barbara spoke out to her music teacher, Miss Inez Davenport. "I told her how sick and tired I was of the inadequate buildings and facilities, and how I wished to hell... something could be done about it."

"Why don't you do something about it?" said Miss Davenport.

So Barbara picked three other student leaders and arranged a meeting. The group included Carrie Stokes, the school president, her twin brother, John, vice president and manager of the school paper and John Watson, a member of the Student Council and the editor of the yearbook. Barbara raised a question: Why had their parents made little progress in forcing the school board to live up to its promises? She suggested that they, the kids, take the lead. "She said we could make a move that would broadcast Prince Edward County all over the world," recalled John Stokes.

Barbara and her friends started attending PTA meetings with the school board to keep track of developments. As usual, when parents asked for a progress report they received the runaround. A few months later, Barbara and the other student leaders brought trusted friends to a secret meeting. Barbara proposed that if things at Moton had not changed by spring, they should lead all the students on a strike. Everyone agreed to the plan.

In February 1951, the county's Board of Supervisors gave the Moton High PTA permission to buy a site for a new black high school. By late April, the purchase had not gone through. The school board told black parents to stay away from monthly meetings and wait to hear from them.

That did it. Barbara and her strike committee sprang into action.

On Monday morning, April 23, 1951, according to plan, the principal of Moton, Boyd Jones, received a phone call. John Watson had gone home on some flimsy excuse and phoned Jones from his mother's private line. Disguising his voice to "sound like a Southern businessman," John told the principal that two of his students were playing hooky and "messing around" at the Greyhound bus terminal downtown. The police would pick the kids up if he didn't get there right away.

The minute the principal left, Barbara went to the auditorium and met with four students. She sent them to every classroom with a message announcing an assembly of the whole school at eleven a.m., and she signed the note the way the principal always did, with the letter *J.*

At eleven o'clock, 450 students and two dozen teachers showed up in the auditorium. Barbara stood before them and asked the teachers to leave. Most of them did. Then she spoke passionately to the students and said it was time they were treated equally with whites. It was up to them to do something about the situation. Barbara said they must march out of school together and stay away until the white community responded to their demands and gave them a decent high school. She assured the kids they wouldn't be punished if they acted together. Besides, the Farmville jail was too small to hold all of them.

Just then, Principal Boyd Jones rushed into the auditorium. He pleaded with the students not to strike. He, too, wanted better conditions for them and had

Some of the Robert R. Moton High School students who participated in the strike. March 1, 1953

appealed to the school board for improvements. He feared losing his job.

Now Barbara respectfully asked him to go to his office. After he left, she and her strike committee ordered the students to stay on the school grounds for the rest of the day. They were not to open books or take part in lessons. Some carried picket signs that they had made in advance and hidden. The signs read WE ARE TIRED OF PAPER SHACKS—WE WANT A NEW SCHOOL. Meanwhile, Barbara and the committee tried to see T. J. McIlwaine, the white superintendent of schools.

McIlwaine refused to meet with them. He believed, incorrectly, that Principal Jones had organized the strike. Barbara later said, "We knew we had to do it ourselves, and that if we had asked for adult help before taking the first step, we would have been turned down."

That afternoon, the strike committee invited Reverend L. Francis Griffin to come to the school and give them advice. Griffin was president of the Moton PTA and founder of the local chapter of the NAACP. He sympathized with the strikers but suggested that they seek their parents' approval. They voted no.

Instead, they asked Griffin to give them the names and addresses of the NAACP's lawyers for their region, and they composed a letter.

It read:

"Gentlemen:

"We hate to impose as we are doing, but under the circumstances that we are facing, we have to ask for your help."

The letter summarized the reasons for the walkout.

"You know that this is a very serious matter because we are out of school, there are seniors to be graduated and it can't be done by staying at home. Please we beg you to come down at the first of this week.... We will go into detail when you arrive."

When Barbara went home she announced, "Grandma, I walked out of school this morning and carried 450 students with me."

"Took my breath away," said her grandma, Ma Croner. "You reckon you done the right thing?" she asked.

"I believe so," said Barbara. "Stick with us."

Ma Croner was proud of Barbara and said of her, "She was a country girl, not some flirty thing worrying about her clothes."

The students remained on strike. A few days later, Barbara and the leaders met with McIlwaine at the county courthouse. "Barbara Johns...did a good deal of the talking," McIlwaine recalled. "She was a nice-looking girl, tall and handsome. They were asking questions like why couldn't they go to the white high school, and I had to explain that we have to live by the laws and that it was just a matter of the Virginia statutes. I said we were going to get them a better school as soon as we could."

Barbara and the others left in disgust.

On the third day of the strike, students arrived at school in buses, but they didn't go inside. Instead, they walked up to Reverend Griffin's First Baptist Church to hear two lawyers from the NAACP, Oliver Hill and Spottswood Robinson III, who had traveled from Richmond, Virginia, in response to the students' letter.

"The kids were so well disciplined and had such high morale and expressed themselves so well," recalled Hill. "We didn't have the nerve to break their hearts."

The lawyers told them that the only way the NAACP could get involved would be if the students sued for the end of segregation as part of Marshall's overall plan. And their parents had to support the legal action.

"It seemed like reaching for the moon," said Barbara. "It was all pretty hard to grasp. But we had great faith in Mr. Robinson and Mr. Hill."

On May 23, 1951, a month after the strike had begun, Robinson filed a suit at the federal courthouse in Richmond, Virginia, on behalf of 117 Moton students who asked that the school segregation laws be struck down. The first person who signed was Dorothy E. Davis, a fourteen-year-old ninth grader. So the case was titled *Davis v. County School Board of Prince Edward County*.

"We didn't pick the Prince Edward County Case," said Hill, "it just developed, and we just went to their rescue."

A few days later Principal Jones was fired.

Barbara's family received threats against her and sent her to Montgomery, Alabama, for her own safety. She stayed there with her uncle Vernon Johns and finished high school. Some people spread a rumor that Johns, a minister and powerful civil rights leader in the community, had instigated the strike.

Barbara's grandpa disagreed. He said, "She had that grit in her herself."

7. PLAYING FOR KEEPS

SEGREGATION was viewed as a well-established southern custom by most whites in Virginia. When the trial for *Davis v. County School Board of Prince Edward County* began on February 25, 1952, Reverend Griffin and a group from Prince Edward County packed the courtroom. Griffin said, "Our people were very enthused—they had hopes that this one trial would settle it all." The NAACP lawyers, Hill and Robinson, weren't so sure. They had tried dozens of cases throughout Virginia and had won some improvements in black schools. But now, in Richmond, with Thurgood Marshall's encouragement, they were suing to end segregated education.

Their opponents, Attorney General James Lindsay Almond, Jr., and lawyers Archibald Gerard Robertson and T. Justin Moore, believed strongly in segregation.

"We all knew that these guys were going to be playing for keeps," said NAACP lawyer Robert Carter, who had come from the New York office to join the team. "They were out to cut our throats—and we, theirs."

NAACP attorneys Spottswood Robinson III on the left, and Oliver Hill on the right, with their clients George Leakes and Elaine Bowen in court listening to Virginia's attorney examining a witness. 1953

A special three-judge District Court heard the case. All of the judges were life-long Virginians.

On the first day of the trial, Carter accused Superintendent McIlwaine of not offering subjects such as physics, world history, geography and trigonometry at Moton. Why didn't the students also have classes in shorthand and mechanical drawing like the students at the white high school? McIlwaine claimed that the black students had never requested these courses.

Robinson produced photographs and documents showing the terrible condi-

tions at Moton. Thomas Henderson, professor of education and dean of Virginia Union University, gave details about the advantages of Farmville High, a school for whites.

Then Hill called Principal Jones to the stand. Jones testified about the overcrowding at Moton, the shortage of buses, his futile efforts to obtain better equipment.

Hill's opponent cross-examined the principal and asked him if it was true that he had not known about the strike before it happened.

"That's exactly right," answered Jones.

"You had no information whatsoever?"

"That's exactly right."

"You did not instigate it, did you?"

"No, sir, I did not."

On the second day of the trial Carter called on John Julian Brooks, former professor of education at New York University. Brooks spoke about the hurtful effects of school segregation on black children. He also explained that while teaching at an integrated Northern school, he had observed that white children accepted and respected black classmates.

Carter's next witness was M. Brewster Smith, chairman of the psychology department at Vassar College. Smith outlined the evidence proving that segregation harmed black children. He said, "Segregation is… a social and official insult."

Moore, defending the school board, shot back that white Virginians would be insulted if their customs were taken away from them.

Carter then called Isidor Chien as a witness. Chien had taught psychology at City College of New York and had become director of a nonprofit research

Gymnasium at Farmville High School for white students, Prince Edward County, Virginia

group. He and a colleague had sent out a questionnaire on race relations to 849 social scientists. The responses showed overwhelmingly that eminent social scientists had research and experience proving that enforced segregation on racial and religious groups had damaging effects.

Moore attacked Chien during his cross-examination by asking him to spell his last name.

"What kind of name is that?" he asked. "What sort of racial background does that indicate?"

Chien answered, "The name is a poor English version of Hebrew which designates 'charm.'"

"What is your racial background?"

"I think what you want to know is am I Jewish."

"Are you 100 percent Jewish?"

"How do I answer that?"

Then Moore asked Chien if Jews suffered discrimination.

"Yes," he answered.

"Is it your view that that has resulted in the Jew feeling any inferiority as to status?"

"Yes, sir."

"You really believe that?"

Classroom at Robert R. Moton High School, Farmville, Virginia

Toilets at Robert R. Moton High School, Farmville, Virginia

"I not only believe it, I have evidence to that effect," said Chien. "But this is to a much less marked degree than in the case of the Negro."

Even Reverend Griffin testified about the strike. He said that before filing the lawsuit, the Moton PTA had received no commitment from the school board to build a new school.

Finally, Kenneth Clark took the stand. Once again he spoke about the results of his psychological tests using dolls. He had not given the tests to the Moton High students because of their age. Instead, he had interviewed fourteen of them. They all viewed their school as "a symbol of some stigma" and believed that the white school was better than theirs.

On the following day, Moore asked Clark if his attendance at Howard, a black university in Washington, D.C., had made him feel inferior. Clark had grown up in New York City and said that at Howard he became aware "of what it really meant to be a Negro in America." For the first time, he had been turned away from a restaurant. So he had led a group of students on a march to the Capitol "to see if we could not get them to treat us like loyal Americans."

Clark concluded that segregated black students in Virginia could never obtain an equal education even if the facilities and equipment were the same. He said, "I think it is the desire of a Negro to be a human being and to be treated as a human being without regard to skin color."

On the third day, the defense began its case. The chairman of the Prince Edward school board boasted that they were making progress in planning a new high school for black students. A Richmond architect discussed his blueprints for the school and claimed that he had been working on them at the time of the strike.

Superintendent McIlwaine took the stand and admitted that inequalities between the white high school and Moton existed but they were being corrected.

The state's superintendent of instruction predicted that ending segregation in schools would be "a catastrophe." He said, "You cannot legislate custom."

Three psychologists followed as witnesses. Professor Henry Garrett of Columbia University in New York City appeared last. "We were scared to death when we saw him in the courthouse," recalled Carter. Garrett had taught Kenneth Clark and his wife, Mamie, and had a "formidable reputation." Out in the hallway, Garrett told Clark that he had agreed to testify because the state officials promised him they were definitely going to make the schools equal.

But on the witness stand, Garrett said, "the principle of separation in education…is long and well established in American life." As examples he cited parochial schools for Catholic children, Hebrew schools for Jewish children and special classes for slow learners. He sneered at Chien's questionnaire about the damaging effects of segregation. In closing, Garrett said, "the Negro student at the high school level will get a better education in a separate school than he will in mixed schools."

On the fifth and final day of the trial, Attorney General Almond said that separation with equal facilities was legal and morally right. The people of Virginia were not prepared to accept integrated schools. If the court handed down a decree to desegregate, Virginians would simply close their public schools.

One week later, on March 7, 1952, the court handed down its decision and ruled against the plaintiffs. Virginia law allowed the state to keep separate schools for black and white children. The law had been in effect for more than eighty years. The judges wrote that they found "no harm or injury to either race." They agreed, however, that the high school for black children was unequal. They ordered the Prince Edward School Board to quickly equalize school buildings, equipment, curriculum and transportation.

"There was never any doubt about the outcome of the trial," Hill said later. "We were trying to build a record for the Supreme Court."

Thurgood Marshall was thrilled. The Supreme Court had already agreed to review his appeals for the South Carolina and Topeka cases. In fall 1952, he appealed the Virginia decision as well. Now all three cases from different parts of the United States would be heard together, so the court's ruling would apply to the whole nation.

8. MAD AT EVERYONE

THURGOOD Marshall began to prepare his legal team for the argument in the Supreme Court. But the court surprised him and asked him to add two more school cases. One of them came from the nation's capital, Washington, D.C. It had started years before with a black barber named Gardner Bishop.

On a Sunday morning in the 1930s, Bishop had taken his four-year-old daughter, Judine, for a walk. Passing a whites-only playground, Bishop dared to enter with Judine and pushed his little girl on a swing. A policeman came along and ordered them to leave. The cop pointed to the sign restricting the playground to whites. Bishop sarcastically said that his daughter couldn't read. Because of his smart-aleck remark the policeman took him down to the station and fined him ten dollars. Bishop raged with anger.

By 1947, Judine, a teenager, attended Browne Junior High School for blacks. The old, overcrowded school had double and triple sessions to accommodate all the students. "When he [her father] found out that we were attending school on a part-time basis," recalled Judine, "he became terribly upset. He decided he was going to do something about it." Eliot Junior High for whites in their neighborhood was half full. With the growing black population in Washington, many white families had fled to the suburbs or had put their children into private schools. Bishop and other furious parents asked why their children couldn't go to Eliot.

In the spring of 1947, the president of the Browne PTA filed a suit against the superintendent of schools in the name of her daughter, Marguerite Carr. Bishop attended a PTA meeting, but he resented the more educated "upper-crust blacks." He said, "We knew the case wasn't going to work, but nobody asked us what we thought because we were nothin'! Nobody gave us a chance to speak. What we wanted was relief, not lawsuits with $500 fees for the lawyers."

Bishop formed a Consolidated Parents Group. "We were mad at everyone—the whites, the highfalutin' blacks, the Board of Education—everyone."

One day he piled Judine and forty other students from Browne into taxis that black cabdrivers had volunteered for the occasion. The destination was a weekly meeting of the Board of Education. The group did not have an appointment. Bishop barged in and announced, "These are children from the Browne Junior High School, and there's not going

to be a one of them…at that school tomorrow, so I just wanted to explain who was doin' it and why."

The board members listened to him but didn't take him seriously. However, that night Bishop followed through on his words and organized a protest. The next day almost all of the 1,800 students who attended Browne either stayed home or went to school to protest with picket signs. They demanded better schools. They wanted half-empty white schools to be turned over to them. The strike continued for two months, but without results.

Then, in February 1948, Bishop went to a NAACP meeting led by Charles Houston, a civil rights lawyer and profes-

Charles Hamilton Houston seated at desk. November 1939

sor at Howard who had taught Thurgood Marshall. Bishop introduced himself to Houston and told him about the problem. "I'd like to help," said Houston.

That night they went to Houston's house and started talking. "He wanted to know everything about us," recalled Bishop. "He seemed terribly concerned." Houston asked Bishop how much money the Consolidated Parents Group had in their treasury. "Fourteen dollars," said Bishop. "Well, you've got yourself a lawyer," said Houston. Houston then arranged to end the strike with the understanding that he would file lawsuits to fight for equality for black school children in Washington.

Bishop and Houston began to work closely together. Houston explained that the District of Columbia was not a state. Therefore, the Fourteenth Amendment requiring states to grant equal rights to all citizens did not apply. But Houston forged on and sued for improvement at every level of education, from kindergarten to high school.

Bishop gathered names on petitions. He arranged fund-raising rallies. As a result, small changes came about. A white high school that was only 60 percent full was converted to a black high school to replace the one that was overcrowded. In 1949, Houston suffered a heart attack. From his hospital bed, he encouraged Bishop to keep fighting. Just as they had predicted, the Court of Appeals for the District of Columbia ruled against Marguerite Carr in the case filed by her mother. In February 1950, the court decided that segregated schools were constitutional.

As Houston lay dying, he advised Bishop to meet his colleague James Madison Nabrit, Jr., a professor of law at Howard University. Nabrit had been assisting Marshall and the Fund since the 1940s. He could take over the lawsuits to win better schools for blacks in Washington. Bishop hesitated. "Nabrit was a big shot," he said, "and I didn't know him."

Bishop continued his crusade despite his doubts. At the first meeting, Nabrit told Bishop he would not take on the lawsuit. It would be a waste of time to pursue equal schools for blacks. But if Bishop could gather a group of plaintiffs to sue against school segregation itself, he would handle the case. They shook hands and Nabrit became Bishop's lawyer.

On September 11, 1950, Bishop led eleven black children to the new John Philip Sousa Junior High School. The sleek

Top: John Philip Sousa Junior High School, Washington, D.C. 1950
Bottom: Classroom at Shaw Junior High School, Washington, D.C. 1950

"Inadequate cafeteria facilities" at Shaw Junior High School, Washington, D.C. 1950

glass and brick building was located across the street from a golf course. The school had forty-two classrooms, a huge auditorium, a gymnasium, basketball courts and a playground. Some of the classrooms were not even in use. Bishop asked the principal to enroll the children. The principal refused. So the children sued to be admitted.

One of the students was a twelve-year-old boy named Spottswood Thomas Bolling, Jr. While the suit was being filed and tried, he and the other kids had to go back to their school, Shaw Junior High. Shaw was forty-eight years old and stood across the street from a pawnbroker's shop. The science lab consisted of one Bunsen burner and a bowl of goldfish.

Bolling's mother, a widow, agreed to list her son's name first as a plaintiff. In early 1951, Nabrit filed a suit against C. Melvin Sharpe, president of the Board of Education of the District of Columbia. The case was titled *Bolling et al. v. Sharpe*. Nabrit based his case solely on an argument that segregated schools were unconstitutional and violated the right to liberty guaranteed by the Fifth Amendment.

There were obvious disparities between Washington, D.C., schools for blacks and

those for whites, but in *Bolling et al. v. Sharpe* the plaintiffs were not suing for equality but for an end to segregation.

In April 1951, Nabrit brought his lawsuit on behalf of Spottswood Bolling, Jr., to the United States District Court. His opponent, the Washington school board, argued that the case should be thrown out. Judge Walter M. Bastian agreed. The school board had asserted that Bolling and the other black children already benefited from the privilege of attending a junior high school. It seemed a ridiculous argument. This meant that the board believed that students at Shaw Junior High clearly enjoyed the educational opportunities which their science equipment, a Bunsen burner and bowl of goldfish, afforded them. In Washington, D.C., segregated schools were legal, however, and Nabrit had not raised the issue of inequality of schools.

Nabrit immediately prepared to appeal his case. In October 1952, while he waited for a hearing before the United States Court of Appeals, he received a phone call from a clerk at the Supreme Court. Chief Justice Fred Vinson wanted Nabrit to petition the Court to have his case brought up with Thurgood Marshall's three school cases. Nabrit wasn't sure he was ready, but he knew this was an order. He said, "We had nothing to lose by an outright assault on segregation."

Opposite top: Empty classroom, Shaw Junior High School, Washington, D.C. 1950
Opposite bottom left: "Inadequate cafeteria facilities," Shaw Junior High School, Washington, D.C. 1950
Opposite bottom center: Home economics room at Shaw Junior High School, Washington, D.C. 1950
Opposite bottom right: Empty classroom, John Philip Sousa Junior High School, Washington, D.C. 1950

9. "WE ARE ALL AMERICAN"

AT the last minute, the Supreme Court added two more school segregation cases for argument. The lawsuits came from Delaware, a border state. Delaware was one of five states lying between the North and the South during the Civil War and was considered middle ground. Justice Tom Clark said, "We felt it was much better to have representative cases from different parts of the country. We consolidated them and made *Brown* the first so that the whole question would not smack of being a purely Southern one."

One of the Delaware lawsuits involved Ethel Louise Belton, a tenth grader, who went to Howard High School in Wilmington. Although Ethel lived in the suburb of

Ethel Louise Belton at Claymont High School, Claymont, Delaware. May 31, 1954

Claymont High School Building, Claymont, Delaware. March 12, 1926

Clayton, she had to go to Howard, a black school downtown. To reach the school she walked a mile to catch a city bus, rode for ten miles, then walked four blocks. "We passed three white high schools on the way," she said. "I had a cardiac condition and that was a lot of walking and climbing hills."

Ethel had been born with six holes in her heart. "I've always been sickly," she explained. "That's why my mother fought so hard to get me in a school close to home." Clayton, the local well-equipped school for whites, had an enrollment of 400, whereas Howard had 1,300. Clayton offered courses such as public speaking,

economics and Spanish—classes unavailable at Howard. And Clayton's extracurricular activities ranged from square dancing and an art club to driver's education and secretarial training.

"Howard didn't have business courses," recalled Ethel, "so two times a week, after school, I walked fifteen blocks to Carver Vocational School to take typing and shorthand. Both nights I went home alone. Some nights it was cold and dark."

Ethel longed to go to Clayton. "Even in tenth grade I hoped to enroll," she said. Like Spottswood Bolling, Jr., in Washington, D.C., and Barbara Johns in Farmville, Virginia, she dared to act. In March 1951, Ethel, age fifteen, met with Louis Lorenzo Redding, Delaware's first black lawyer. Her mother and other black parents from the community of Clayton joined her. Redding, a graduate of Harvard Law School, had begun working with Jack Greenberg, a lawyer at Thurgood Marshall's Fund.

Redding urged the parents to ask the State Board of Education to admit their children to the local white high school. The parents tried and were turned down. So Ethel and nine other plaintiffs filed a suit against Francis Gebhart, the school board president for New Castle County, Delaware.

Ethel's mother said, "We are all American, and when the state sets up separate schools for certain people of a separate color, then I and others are made to feel ashamed and embarrassed."

Meanwhile, in Hockessin, Delaware, a mother named Sarah Bulah also fought segregation. Mrs. Bulah adored her adopted daughter, Shirley Barbara. Every day she drove eight-year-old Shirley down to the one-room schoolhouse for blacks in the village of Hockessin, two miles away from their home. In bad weather, she waited with Shirley until the teacher

Shirley Barbara Bulah, age eight

arrived. A bus for white children passed right by the Bulahs' front door and took them to "the pretty little school up on the hill." Why couldn't the bus stop for Shirley? And why wasn't there a school bus for black children? This angered Mrs. Bulah even more than the differences between the two schools.

So she wrote a letter to the Department of Public Instruction for the State of Delaware. Weeks passed without a response. Then she wrote to Governor Elbert N. Carvel. He replied that they had no "transportation facilities" for Shirley's school. The governor suggested that Mrs. Bulah apply for a "private allowance" according to Rule 18 in a booklet that he enclosed. But Rule 18 applied only to families who lived farther away from the schoolhouse.

Undaunted, Mrs. Bulah sent more letters. The state superintendent of the Department of Public Instruction finally answered that they had reviewed her case. Bussing was part of the school program. Since the state required separate schools for white and black children, Shirley could not ride on a bus serving a white school.

Mrs. Bulah went to see lawyer Louis Redding from Thurgood Marshall's Fund. "He said he wouldn't help me get a Jim Crow bus to take my girl to any Jim Crow school," she recalled. "But if I was interested in sendin' her to an integrated school, why, then maybe he'd help."

That night Redding visited Mrs. Bulah and her husband, Fred, at their house. He wanted to be sure that they understood the risks involved if he took their case. They remained determined. Redding dictated a letter that Mrs. Bulah signed requesting Shirley's admission to the "pretty little" white school. She sent the letter to the chairman of the local school board, and it was forwarded to the state board. The board informed Mrs. Bulah that her request went against the law. So she sued.

None of the black people in Hockessin joined the lawsuit or supported her. Even her minister, Reverend Martin Luther Kilson of the Chippey African Union Methodist Church said, "I was

Colored School, Hockessin, Delaware. 1941

for segregation. These folks around here would rather have a colored teacher. They didn't want to be mixed up with no white folks. All we wanted was a bus for the colored."

Nevertheless, Sarah and Fred Bulah stood firm. Redding filed the lawsuit in Wilmington. Again he named Francis B. Gebhart, a member of the State Board of Education, as the defendant. The two Delaware cases were combined and called *Belton v. Gebhart* and *Bulah v. Gebhart.*

Redding was all set to challenge the state's racist policies. He headed for court feeling that he had a good chance of winning.

10. IN THE MINDS OF CHILDREN

THE trial for the Delaware school cases was scheduled for October 22, 1951. Jack Greenberg, a member of Thurgood Marshall's staff, assisted Louis Redding. They had teamed up the year before and had won a case integrating the University of Delaware.

"Early in August I began assembling a group of expert witnesses," wrote Greenberg. "We needed someone to survey the schools, and once more there were social scientists. I put together a great crew."

Kenneth Clark agreed to testify. Also Dr. Frederic Wertham, a famous psychiatrist who ran a free mental health clinic in Harlem, a black neighborhood in New York City. Greenberg and Wertham decided that it would be a good idea to interview some of the children from Delaware before the trial. A member of the Wilmington NAACP escorted children ranging in age from nine to sixteen to New York on the train. Eight of the students were black, and five were white. Greenberg met them at Pennsylvania Station and took them to the clinic.

"The first time they came up," said Greenberg, "I thought I would treat them to dinner in a Chinese restaurant, a new experience for all of them. That turned out to be a big mistake." The children loved the food and ordered "the most expensive dishes on the menu." Greenberg wondered if he'd have enough money to pay the bill.

When the trial began, the cases were heard in the Court of Chancery. A chancery court is a court of equity: A chancellor presides and settles disputes, determining what is fair. The chancellor was Collins J. Seitz. He had ruled in favor of Greenberg and Redding when they had argued against segregation at the University of Delaware, so the lawyers felt hopeful.

Greenberg called on Kenneth Clark as his first witness. Clark reported the results of conducting his doll tests with forty-one Delaware children: "Three out of every four youngsters—who when asked the question, 'Which of these dolls is likely to act bad?' picked the brown doll," he said. "I think we have rather clear-cut evidence of rather deep damage to the self-esteem of these youngsters, a feeling of inferiority."

Dr. Wertham testified for more than an hour. "He captivated the courtroom," recalled Greenberg. "The Viennese accent helped, but the impact came from what he had to say."

African American children in classroom, from the NAACP Collection of Photographs of Schools and Activities to End Segregation. 1940–1960

Dr. Wertham spoke about his interviews with the children individually and in groups. The black children had opened up and talked about feelings they couldn't comfortably discuss with their parents. They felt unhappy about the long bus rides. "I travel thirty miles a day to school," said one of the students. "The white high school is twelve blocks away."

A thirteen-year-old said, "When we get on the bus, the white children [outside] look at us and laugh."

Another girl said, "When you sit with the white people, they look at you so hard."

A boy added, "If I have to go to segregated schools all the time, I won't know how to react to different people in life.... [You] have to be so careful about what you say, how you act. Seems you don't have a chance to act normal [and] natural."

The children confided that they mainly experienced prejudice from "the plain Americans." Dr. Wertham realized the phrase referred to Anglo-Saxon Protestants. "The others are foreigners," the children had said. "They're much nicer to us. They treat us better—the Poles, the Italians, the Jews, the Catholics, the Germans." As examples they reported that some Catholic schools accepted black children, and some Italian restaurants served them and their families. One sixteen-year-old girl told how she and a friend had gone job-hunting during the summer but had been turned down by a restaurant owner who said that he "did not hire colored dishwashers."

Wertham recounted terrible incidents of prejudice he had heard. One child told him that in her class the white boys wanted to tie up black children and make them work. "The boys say that they [the Negro children] should work and we should play," she had revealed. "I guess they got that from the comic books."

In closing, Dr. Wertham said that the state perpetuated school segregation. Physical differences in schools didn't matter, he thought. Even if Professor Albert Einstein were teaching black children in a magnificent school built of marble, segregation would cause harm. "Most of the children we have examined interpret segregation... as punishment," he said. "Whether the state of Delaware wants to punish these children, has nothing to do with it. I am only testifying about what is in the minds of the children."

After three days of testimony, Chancellor Seitz wanted to see for himself how the black schools compared to the white schools. With his clerk and the opposing lawyers, he visited Howard High School and the Carver vocational annex that Ethel Belton attended. The urinals at Howard were not working and the stench was overpowering. Claymont School was clearly "vastly superior," observed Seitz.

But the contrast of the schools in Hockessin startled him even more. "No. 29 [the white school] is so beautifully situated that the view immediately catches the eye," wrote Seitz in his opinion. "The landscaping is also outstanding." Rosebushes and pine trees bordered the school area. Inside the four-classroom school Seitz noted a nurse's office, a basketball court and an auditorium where young white children performed a dance program. Shirley Barbara Bulah's one-room schoolhouse in the village was a stark contrast. It certainly had no dance classes, no auditorium. Instead of a nurse's office there was just a first-aid kit. As for landscaping, there was not even a tree or a flower.

Five months later, on April 1, 1952, Seitz issued his opinion. "I believe the 'separate but equal' doctrine in education should be rejected," he wrote. "The cold hard fact is that the state in this situation discriminates against Negro children."

Seitz ordered that Shirley Barbara Bulah in Hockessin, and Ethel Louise Belton and the nine other plaintiffs, were to be immediately enrolled at the white schools in their communities.

"Lou Redding and I won the first case ever to order black children admitted to white schools," wrote Greenberg.

"This is the first real victory in our campaign to destroy segregation of American pupils in elementary and high schools," announced Marshall.

"Now," said Greenberg, "we had to hope that the state would appeal, because Delaware would be a great case to take to the Supreme Court."

Delaware's Attorney General, Albert Young, appealed the decision right away. But Redding and Greenberg won again in the Delaware Supreme Court. The court upheld Seitz's ruling, and in the fall black children began attending white schools in Claymont and Hockessin.

Eight-year-old Shirley Barbara felt welcomed by her new white classmates. "They came to my birthday parties at my house, and I went to theirs," she said in an interview with a Wilmington newspaper. "I didn't have to worry about being punched or worry about getting gum in my hair."

Ethel Belton said, "I'm glad I helped start the change in Delaware. The only hurting part is that I didn't get a chance to go [to Clayton].... But it helped my children and others."

When Young filed an appeal with the United States Supreme Court, Greenberg was delighted. "One winning case before the Court would improve the chances of all the cases," he wrote. "Ego was involved too: we wanted *our* case up there."

Hockessin School, Hockessin, Delaware. 1954

11. HELPING MAKE HISTORY

ON the morning of December 9, 1952, four hundred spectators lined the marble corridors of the vast Supreme Court building in Washington, D.C. Many of them had waited there overnight hoping to get a seat. Inside, about three hundred people packed the awe-inspiring room. Half of them were black. Seating was not segregated. The crowd included Reverend DeLaine from Clarendon County, South Carolina. DeLaine had organized the uprising leading to *Briggs v. Elliot*, one of the five cases to be argued. Thurgood Marshall had given him a ticket for the proceedings.

Marshall and his team had been preparing for this battle since August. "Well before we appeared in court," wrote Jack Greenberg, "we anticipated that *Brown* might be a historic case."

At long meetings in Marshall's New York office they had debated their course of action. Marshall listened and challenged everything everyone said. Should they attack segregation head-on? Would any of the Supreme Court Justices be sympathetic to white Southerners and support segregation? How much testimony from social scientists should they use? Would the Supreme Court Justices think

Kenneth Clark's psychological tests using dolls foolish? And if the NAACP won and the Court ordered integration in the schools, how would this ruling be put into effect?

The Fund lawyers often slept in the office, working past midnight on the briefs. "Each brief called for an end to segregation in education," wrote Greenberg. Spottswood Robinson, who had represented the striking students in Virginia, reviewed every draft. Whenever he had more changes for Marshall's secretary to type, she'd shout, "If I have to do this one more time—!" But an older secretary said to her, "I don't know whether you know it, but you're helping make history here tonight. If Mr. Robinson tells you to do that fifty times, you type it!"

Marshall edited the briefs to remove

Spottswood Robinson III (left) and Thurgood Marshall (right) in Washington, D.C.

any "snide cracks" about the opposing lawyers who would be arguing for segregation. Ten days before the Supreme Court date, Marshall and his team traveled to Washington, D.C., and holed up in a suite at the Statler Hotel. They conducted a "dry run" of their arguments at Howard Law School for an audience of students and professors who hurled questions at them. These might be the very questions the justices would ask.

Marshall invited his chief opponent, John W. Davis, to have lunch with him. Some of the NAACP lawyers were puzzled. Marshall explained, "We're both attorneys, we're both civil. It's very important to have a civil relationship with your opponent."

Lunch went well. Davis was courteous and kind. Marshall enjoyed being treated as a peer. As a college student earning money for tuition, he had waited tables in an exclusive club for white Protestants on Chesapeake Bay where his father was the steward of the all-black staff. Now Marshall was being served along with a white Protestant lawyer. Marshall greatly admired Davis, a distinguished older lawyer from Charleston, South Carolina. Davis had argued hundreds of cases before the Supreme Court, more times than any other living lawyer. When Marshall had been a law student at Howard he had cut classes to hear Davis in the Court. "I learned most of my stuff from him," he said.

Now Davis headed a powerful law firm in New York City. His friend Governor James Byrnes of South Carolina had asked him to take *Briggs v. Elliot*. Davis, a confirmed segregationist, had agreed to do it without charging a fee. He felt confident that he would win. In a speech about how to star in the Supreme Court he had said, *"Always go for the jugular vein....* Get right to the heart of your case. And sit down before your time is up."

At noon on the opening day of the oral arguments, the nine justices, wearing robes, took their seats. The lawyers, all men, followed a dress code: They either wore vests or kept their suit jackets buttoned. Davis conformed to an earlier tradition and wore formal morning clothes. The first case on the agenda was *Brown*. Each side had one hour to speak. When a red light flashed, signaling that time was up, a lawyer had to stop even if he was in the middle of a sentence.

At 1:35 p.m., Robert Carter began arguing on behalf of Oliver Brown, his daughter Linda and the nine other plaintiffs from Topeka. By now Linda was ten years old and in fifth grade. She and her younger sister, Terry, still took the long trip to attend Monroe, the school for blacks. Carter told how segregated schools deprived black children of equal educational opportunities. He said, "Separate but equal...should squarely be overruled."

His opponent, Attorney General Paul Wilson, defended Jim Crow schools in Kansas. He disagreed that segregation hurt black children. The court adjourned promptly at 2:00 p.m. for lunch, then reconvened at 2:30 p.m.

After Carter finished his remarks, Marshall went to the lectern to argue *Briggs v. Elliott*. He had been "edgy and irritable" until his turn came. Marshall spoke against South Carolina's practice of segregating schoolchildren on the basis of race. Expert witnesses like Kenneth Clark had testified in the lower court that this practice harmed children. Justice Felix Frankfurter interrupted him and asked how integration would be carried out if it were deemed constitutional. Marshall answered that the details would have to be worked out by local school boards. "It might take six months to do in one place and two months to do it another place."

Davis took his turn and stated that South Carolina was in the process of making schools equal. The evidence of social scientists had nothing to do with constitutional rights. He made fun of Clark's tests using dolls in Clarendon County and said that many "learned authorities" approved of segregation. The practice was ninety years old and he saw no reason for change.

In his rebuttal, Marshall stressed his main argument. "For some reason," he said, "Negroes are taken out of the mainstream of American life....There is nothing involved in this case other than race and color."

He added, "I know in the South, where I spend most of my time, you will see white and colored kids going down the road together to school. They separate and go to different schools, and they come out and they play together. I do not see why there would necessarily be any trouble if they went to school together."

Spottswood Robinson spoke next on behalf of the students who had gone on strike at Moton. Barbara Johns, who had organized the strike, had already graduated from Alabama State Laboratory High School in Montgomery. John Watson, another of the plaintiffs, had graduated

From left to right: Attorneys Harold Boulware, Thurgood Marshall, and Spottswood Robinson III confer at the Supreme Court prior to presenting arguments against segregation in schools during *Brown v. Board of Education*

from Moton and had joined the Air Force. A new black high school was under construction. A new school would not mean equality, however. Barbara Johns, Dorothy Davis, John Watson and the other black students should have been admitted to the white high school, and black students like them should have that opportunity.

The court adjourned and Robinson continued the next day. His opponent, Justin Moore of Richmond, Virginia, argued that the student strike had blocked financing for a new high school for blacks, which wasn't true. "The strike was really inspired by outsiders," he lied. Moore also declared that segregation did not endanger black children. Justice Robert Jackson asked him about the Fourteenth Amendment, which protects the rights of individuals. Moore replied that the Fourteenth Amendment did not cover local matters such as schools.

That afternoon, James Nabrit and his colleague, George Edward Chalmers Hayes, an experienced black lawyer who taught at Howard, began their presentation on behalf of Spottswood Bolling, Jr., and the children of Shaw Junior High.

At 4:30 the session ended, but the following day Hayes carried on. He argued that school segregation in Washington, D.C., was unconstitutional. It violated the Fifth Amendment by denying black children the liberty to attend unsegregated schools. Nabrit spoke and charged that individual liberties of citizens such as the children were provided for in the Bill of Rights.

Their opponent, Milton Korman, said, "Separate public schools had been established in the District [of Columbia] before the Civil War ended and the amendments had been put through. These were slaves who had just been freed.... The District was trying to do its best for these people who had been in bondage. But there was no intention to invite them into their homes or to share their schools." Korman insisted that Shaw Junior High, which was across the street from a pawnbroker's shop, had been established out of a "kindly feeling."

Nabrit rose for the rebuttal. In a stirring speech, he said, "In the heart of the nation's capital, in the capital of democracy, in the capital of the free world, there is no place for a segregated school system."

On Thursday, December 11, Attorney General Albert Young of Delaware spoke first because he had lost in the state courts. He said that chancellor Seitz had acted too quickly in ordering the white schools in Claymont and Hockessin to admit black students. Delaware had every intention of making Howard High School equal to Clayton.

But lawyers Redding and Greenberg pointed out that students like Ethel Belton, who lived in Clayton, would still have a ten-mile bus ride to and from school. Evidence showed that Shirley Barbara and other black children who had started attending integrated schools were getting along with their white classmates.

Greenberg said, "I concluded the argument in the Delaware case, which was also the end of the arguments for all five cases."

On the way out of the Supreme Court Building, Davis was overheard remarking to his colleague from Virginia, "I think we've got it won."

12. WE KNEW WE WERE RIGHT

AFTER the last day of arguments in the Supreme Court, Marshall returned to New York for Christmas. He was exhausted. The other Fund lawyers went back to their practices as they waited for the Court's decision.

Greenberg said, "All we could do was wait."

Meanwhile, on Saturday morning, December 13, 1952, the Justices gathered to discuss the five cases. In keeping with tradition they shook hands, then sat at a long table in the conference room behind the courtroom. Floor-to-ceiling shelves held law books that recorded all of the previous cases.

The rule was that each justice took a turn speaking. Chief Justice Vinson went first. Then they opened up a discussion. No one knows what the justices said at this private conference, but Justices Robert Jackson and Harold Burton took notes that were later made public.

Chief Justice Vinson was not ready to abolish segregation in schools. Perhaps in Washington, D.C., but not in the states. The South Carolina case, *Briggs v. Elliott,* that Marshall had argued troubled him the most. Jackson noted that Vinson said that the court should "not close eyes to the seriousness of problem."

Supreme Court Justices with Chief Justice Fred Vinson at beginning of *Brown* case. 1952 (front row, left to right: Felix Frankfurter, Hugo Black, Fred Vinson, Stanley Reed and William O. Douglas; back row, left to right: Tom Clark, Robert Jackson, Harold Burton and Sherman Minton)

Marshall's opponent Davis had threatened that South Carolina would close their public schools if the Court ordered integration.

Hugo Black, who came from Alabama, wanted to end segregation. "Segregation per se is a violation of the Fourteenth Amendment," he declared. He tried to persuade the other justices to rule against the Jim Crow practice.

Stanley Reed disagreed. Notes on his comments read, "Uphold Seg." He said, "Negroes have not thoroughly assimilated/must try our best to give Negroes benefits. Must start with the

idea that... separation of races is for benefit of both."

Felix Frankfurter deeply opposed segregation. Yet *Brown* presented difficulties. How would the states handle integration in schools? The South should be allowed time to adjust. How much time? Why delay in giving black children their rights? Maybe they should wait and see if South Carolina really improved the black schools and made them equal.

William Douglas knew exactly how he wanted to vote. "Very simple for me," he said at the conference. "*State* can't classify by color for education."

Robert Jackson thought they needed more time to discuss the cases. He wasn't sure that Marshall was right and that racism could be overcome in America by "putting children together."

Burton's diary shows that he supported the black people's struggle for equal rights and wanted to end segregation. "Agree should be done in [as] easy [a] way as possible," he said during the meeting.

Although Tom Clark usually sided with Vinson he was not ready to take a stand on *Brown*. "Think wiser to hold off," he remarked. "Have led states on to believe separate but equal OK."

Sherman Minton from Indiana was prepared to vote. He said, "Segregation in and of itself was unconstitutional."

Frankfurter proposed that they rehear the cases, and everyone agreed. A court date was set for June 1953, then postponed till October. In the meantime, Frankfurter drafted questions for the opposing lawyers: What did the framers of the Fourteenth Amendment intend? Did the Supreme Court have the power to abolish school segregation? If the Court ordered schools to be integrated how would it be handled?

Some members of Marshall's staff regarded the delay as a good sign. Greenberg said, "We thought we had the case basically won. Why would the Court have put questions about remedy if it weren't seriously contemplating a remedy? They were asking us to help figure out...how to do it....We were quite encouraged."

But Robert Carter, an older black lawyer, felt less optimistic. The Court's questions "shook us," he said. "Where we had been 75 percent confident, we now were down to 50 or 55 percent confident. We took it all very seriously...we had a lot to do. It was a very exhilarating time, that summer."

Marshall called scholars around the country to help research. He asked his friend John A. Davis, a professor of political science at Lincoln University, to head the team. Davis came to New York and had a desk and a phone at the Fund office. "I talked with everyone I knew in constitutional history, Reconstruction history, the history of education and black history," he said. "The mood was hectic, driving, disordered and anxious."

Everyone worked late and subsisted on sandwiches and coffee. Alice Stovall, who managed the office, said, "I think we all felt that we might be making history."

On September 8, 1953, a month

before the arguments were to be heard, Chief Justice Vinson died of a heart attack. President Dwight D. Eisenhower nominated a new Chief Justice: Earl Warren, the former governor of California.

Marshall worried about the choice. Warren had been in charge of California's program to put Japanese citizens in internment camps during World War II, an act he later regretted. Marshall hurried to California to check up on Warren. Everyone he spoke to said, "The man was simply great." Warren was known for his honesty, dignity and common sense.

Chief Justice Earl Warren. 1953

At this point the rearguments were postponed again and scheduled for early December. The postponement gave Marshall and his team more time to prepare the brief, which had to be submitted in November. Marshall gathered nearly a hundred scholars and lawyers for a three-day conference to discuss aspects of the Court's questions. In October, he held another conference with only his inner circle to go over historical evidence. "I never worked for harder taskmasters," recalled historian John Franklin.

"I never had so much fun in my life as during those sessions," said Charles L. Black, Jr., a young professor at Columbia University. Black worked on the final brief and seemed to relish being part of the team. He didn't complain when his words were rewritten or discarded. He said, "Everything was torn to pieces."

Meanwhile, Marshall and other members of the staff gave speeches to raise money to pay for research, travel and printing the brief. The black press started a campaign to get contributions with the slogan, "Dollar or more will open the door." Churches, black businesses and the black American Teachers Association made donations. Branches of the NAACP in Virginia and South Carolina sent thousands of dollars. Secretaries and volunteers in the Fund's national office in New York City on West Fortieth Street worked in shifts of fifteen to twenty hours a day, seven days a week, without extra pay.

June Shagaloff, Marshall's assistant, went to Delaware to study recently desegregated schools to help form a plan for integration in answer to one of the Court's questions. "We knew we were right," she said. "Everybody believed what we were doing."

However, the opposing lawyers who were defending segregation also thought they were right. John W. Davis headed the research team at his New York law office. He sent law students to the New York Public Library and to the Library of Congress in Washington to examine congressional debates. They found no evidence that the framers of the Fourteenth Amendment intended to outlaw segregated schools. A colleague said, "Mr. Davis felt…he had the case won."

The Virginia brief stated that separate schools were "in the best interest of both races."

Justice Reed had expressed the same opinion at the secret meeting the year before. What would the Court decide?

Editorial page cartoon, "Our Thanksgiving Day Prayer," *Baltimore Afro-American,* November 28, 1953

13. WE, TOO, ARE EQUAL

AT 1:00 a.m. on December 7, 1953, Arthur J. Smith, an elderly black man, stood first on line at the front door of the Supreme Court. At 2:00 a.m., a Howard law student joined him. By daybreak Reverend DeLaine of South Carolina, the organizer of *Briggs v. Elliott,* showed up. He told a reporter for the *Baltimore Afro-American*, "There were times when I thought I would go out of my mind because of this case....I feel it was worth it. I have a feeling that the Supreme Court is going to end segregation."

Later in the morning, Marshall's mother, Norma, and his wife, Vivian (Buster), sat in reserved seats. Arguments began at 1:05 p.m. Marshall and Robinson combined the Virginia and South Carolina cases, and Robinson spoke first. He declared that the framers of the Fourteenth Amendment had intended to achieve "complete legal equality" for Negroes. School segregation had to be struck down.

Marshall spoke next and focused on Supreme Court rulings that protected individual rights. But the Justices didn't want to hear that. They questioned him about history, which had been Robinson's specialty, and Marshall fumbled.

People lining up at the Supreme Court, hoping to get one of the fifty available seats to hear arguments in the *Brown* case. December 1953

Then Marshall's opponent, Davis, went to the lectern. Eloquently, he argued that Congress had intended to keep schools segregated when they passed the Fourteenth Amendment. He warned the Court that there would be a problem if schools were desegregated in areas like Clarendon County, South Carolina, where there were 2,800 black pupils and 300 white ones. If the children were to be "comingled, who knows how that would best be done?" he asked. "Would that make the children any happier? Would they learn any more quickly?" Tears ran down his cheeks as he concluded.

One of Greenberg's colleagues said, "That sonofabitch cries in every case he argues."

"He was old," said Marshall. "And he cried. Real tears while he was arguing."

The following day Marshall came back in top form. "Thurgood's rebuttal was his best argument ever," wrote Greenberg. First, Marshall attacked Davis's argument that it was "reasonable" to separate the races in school. Then he addressed Davis's claim that blacks were seeking "racial prestige" by going to school with whites.

"Exactly correct," said Marshall. "Ever since the Emancipation Proclamation, the Negro has been trying to get... the same status as anybody else regardless of race." In conclusion, he said the South wanted to continue school segregation to keep "the people who were formerly in slavery...as near that stage as is possible. Now is the time," said Marshall, "that this Court should make it clear that that is not what our Constitution stands for."

Next, the *Brown* case was discussed briefly because Topeka had begun to integrate elementary schools.

On the third day, the District of Columbia case came up. Milton Korman, who was defending segregation, said that the school board had not changed its position.

Nabrit responded emotionally. He said, "Our Constitution has no provision across it that all men are equal but that white men are more equal than others. Under this statute and under this country, under this Constitution, and under the protection of this Court, we believe that we, too, are equal."

Greenberg argued last in the Delaware case. He said that integration was under way in Wilmington, but there was still a state law segregating schools. His clients, Shirley Barbara Bulah and Ethel Belton, remained "under a cloud." What if they were segregated again? Justice Frankfurter snapped, "I am glad to get your observations, but I do not think the nature of the issues had been changed."

During the half-hour recess for lunch, the NAACP lawyers huddled. They decided to put Marshall on instead of Greenberg for the wrap-up. In closing, Marshall gave a powerful summation. He noted that the four state cases had been consolidated because they had the same constitutional issue. The question, he told the Court, was "whether or not the wishes of these [segregationist] states shall prevail or whether our Constitution shall prevail." And at 2:40 p.m., the Court adjourned. Their ruling was not due till spring.

At the justices' private conference on Saturday morning, December 12, Chief

Justice Warren spoke first. "I don't remember having any great doubts about which way it should go," he recalled years later. "The only way the case could be decided was clear. The question was *how* the decision was to be reached." Segregation of Negro schoolchildren had to be ended.

The justices, however, expressed conflicting views. Warren said, "We decided not to make up our minds on that first conference day, but to talk it over, from week to week, dealing with different aspects of it—in groups, over lunches, in conference. It was too important to hurry it."

14. THE GREATEST VICTORY

WHILE Marshall waited for the Court's decision, he went on the road giving speeches at NAACP fund-raisers. The legal team had run up huge bills, and they needed more donations. In January, at a national meeting of black publishers in Tuskegee, Alabama, Marshall thanked the publishers for placing special ads soliciting contributions to the NAACP, which had brought in almost eighteen thousand dollars. On an upbeat note, he predicted that the Supreme Court would end segregation.

Unbeknownst to anyone, the Justices started voting secretly at their Saturday conferences in late February. According to notes taken by Justice Frankfurter, they still argued as they thrashed out aspects of the case. But they had agreed that no word ought to leak out before they made their decision.

On March 1, Warren was confirmed as Chief Justice and sworn in.

Meanwhile, Marshall traveled around the country gathering pledges for financial support. At an event in Charlottesville, Virginia, he told the audience that "come Hell or high water, we are going to be free by '63." He asked them to remember President Lincoln's Emancipation Proclamation and said, "On freedom's 100th anniversary we will be free as we should have been in 1863."

In April, there was still no announcement of a ruling. Marshall wondered if there would be more delays. When would the Court make a decision? Would there be dissenting opinions from some of the justices?

On Sunday, May 16, Marshall spoke in Mobile, Alabama. The next day he planned to go to Los Angeles. But that night he received a phone call telling him to change his schedule and go to Washington instead. Marshall never revealed the identity of the caller, but he caught the next flight to D.C.

On Monday, May 17, Marshall went to the Supreme Court and sat in the lawyers' section. The nine justices appeared and took their seats. At 12:52 p.m., Chief Justice Warren said, "I have for announcement the judgment and opinion of the Court in No. 1—*Oliver Brown et al. v. Board of Education of Topeka.*" Warren began reading the decision on the four state cases in a "firm, clear, unemotional" voice.

"In these days it is doubtful that any child may reasonably be expected to succeed in life if he is denied the opportunity of an education...a right which must be made available to all on equal terms," he said. "To separate [black children] from others of similar age and qualifications solely because of their race generates a feeling of inferiority as to their status in the community that may affect their hearts and minds in a way unlikely ever to be undone."

"We conclude," he said, and looked up to add the word "unanimously," "that in the field of public education the doctrine of 'separate but equal' has no place. Separate educational facilities are inherently unequal."

A muffled gasp went through the room.

Marshall later said that when he heard those words, "I was so happy I was numb."

Warren added that the court would schedule time in the fall term to hear from the attorney generals throughout the South and the rest of the United States concerning means for putting the ruling into effect. Then Warren read the opinion on the District of Columbia case, *Bolling v. Sharpe.* "In view of our decision that the Constitution prohibits the states from maintaining racially segregated public schools, it would be unthinkable that the same Constitution would impose a lesser duty on the Federal Government."

The justices filed out of the court, and reporters who had been standing in the back of the room swarmed Marshall. Before answering any questions he turned to his Washington, D.C., colleagues, Nabrit and Hayes, who had argued the *Bolling v. Sharpe* case, and said, "We hit the jackpot."

To a reporter for the *Afro* he said, "It is the greatest victory we ever had…the thing that is gratifying to me is that it was unanimous and on our side."

Reporters dashed to the pressroom and sent out bulletins.

Marshall ran out into the hall to a pay phone and called Greenberg with the news. Greenberg, at the NAACP office in New York, called other members of the

From left to right: Attorneys George E. C. Hayes, Thurgood Marshall and James Nabrit on the steps of the Supreme Court Building congratulating each other on the *Brown* decision. May 17, 1954

staff. Then, as photographers snapped pictures, Marshall raced down the steps to catch a plane to New York.

In Topeka, Linda Brown's mother, Leola, was doing the family ironing when she heard the news over the radio. She said, "All the kids were in school, my husband had gone to work and I'm at home doing that. And when it came over [the radio] and they said...segregation had been defeated, was outlawed, oh, boy, I think I was doing the dance there at home all by myself. I was so elated. I could hardly wait until my kids and my husband got home to relate to them."

When Oliver Brown heard the Court's ruling he told a reporter for the *Kansas City Times*, "I feel that this decision holds a better future, not for one family, but for every child indicated." Linda attended Curtis Junior High, an integrated school. She said, "The media started coming and wanting to take pictures. It was really unbelievable that they were here to see me. It was exciting to all the children to have media at school and photographers taking pictures of the classes." Up till then she had been unaware of the ongoing litigation. "I really didn't even think about it that much," she said. But she added, "I'm proud that the decision carries my name."

McKinley Burnett, president of the Topeka branch of the NAACP, who had invited Oliver and Linda Brown to a meeting four years before, said, "I'm completely overwhelmed....It makes me feel that I'm an American citizen in the true sense of the word." He said that although the court had not decided "the time and means for abolishing segregation," it had "broken the back of segregation." That night the NAACP of Topeka held a victory party at Monroe School, the black school Linda Brown and her sisters had attended.

In Washington, D.C., Spottswood Bolling, Jr., fifteen and a high school

Spottswood Thomas Bolling Jr. and his mother Sarah Bolling in Washington, D.C. May 17, 1954

sophomore, read the front-page news with his mother. She congratulated him on the headline in the *Washington Post*: "Separate but Equal Doctrine is Thrown Out. Equal Education for All."

Ethel Belton, seventeen, had just graduated from Howard University when she heard the "good news." She said, "I felt kind of great. It wasn't everybody who took a stand like my mother and me. I feel very privileged to be a part of the change in Delaware."

Barbara Johns, who had led the Moton strike, was attending Spelman College in Atlanta when the Court rendered its deci-

Joan Marie Johns at graduation from the new Robert R. Moton High School, Farmville, Virginia. 1955

sion. Her younger sister Joan, who had taken part in the strike and was now a student at the new Moton High School in Farmville, called her on the phone. Joan said, "Barbara was so excited she shouted with happiness. We never knew it [the strike] would end up being a historical event."

In South Carolina, Eliza Briggs said, "I wonder why a little town like Clarendon changed history." Her son Harry Briggs, Jr., was thirteen and attending Sumerton Elementary School. Her husband, Harry Briggs, the plaintiff for whom the case was named, had moved to Miami, Florida, to find work because no one in Sumerton would hire him after he had signed the petition.

That night in New York, Marshall celebrated with his entire staff. "We always had parties...after winning," he said, "but that was the best. I thought I was going to win but not unanimously."

His opponent, John W. Davis, called him to congratulate him on his victory.

"I beat him," said Marshall, "but you can't name many people who did." During the festivities Marshall toasted Kenneth Clark to honor him for his contribution to the case. People at the party kept saying the NAACP's work was done and soon all the schools in the nation

Demonstrating a voting machine at Howard High School, Wilmington, Delaware. 1954

would be integrated. One staff member said that they "just sat there looking at one another. The only emotion we felt at that moment was awe—every one of us felt it."

"It was all so awesome," wrote Greenberg. "We still didn't know what it meant or where it would lead."

After midnight Marshall's mood turned somber, and he said, "I don't want any of you to fool yourselves, it's just begun, the fight has just begun."

15. HOW THINGS WORKED IN AMERICA

SOON after the court's ruling on May 17, 1954, Barbara Johns's sister Joan and her parents left Virginia for a weekend visit with relatives in Washington, D.C. Joan's younger brothers stayed with Grandma Croner. During the night, Joan's family's house went up in flames. Her uncle spotted the fire and wakened the Croners. But it was too late. The house burned down. When Joan and her parents returned, the house "was in ashes," she said. "It was horrible. We were all just in tears." Although the fire was investigated, "nothing came of it," said Joan. "My parents weren't too surprised." They suspected the fire had been set because Joan and Barbara were plaintiffs in the case that was part of *Brown*.

Southerners blasted the court's decision. Governor Thomas B. Stanley of Virginia urged citizens to remain calm. But the state's Senator Harry Byrd said, "We are facing a crisis of the first magnitude."

Governor James F. Byrnes of South Carolina said, "South Carolina will not now nor for some years to come mix white and colored children in our schools."

Governor Herman Talmadge of Georgia exclaimed, "I do not believe in Negroes

Left: Happy students in New Orleans, Louisiana. 1954
Right: Myrtha Trotter at Claymont High School, Claymont, Delaware. May 31, 1954

and whites, associating with each other either socially or in school systems, and as long as I am governor, it won't happen."

Black communities cheered the landmark decision. Robert Johnson, a history professor at Virginia Union University said, "This is a most exciting moment. A lot of us haven't been breathing for the past nine months.... Today the students reacted as if a heavy burden had been lifted from their shoulders. They see a new world opening up for them and those that follow them."

Sara Lightfoot, who grew up to be a writer, sociologist and professor of education at Harvard, was ten when she heard the news. "Jubilation, optimism and hope filled my home," she wrote. "And for the first time I saw tears in my father's eyes." He said to Sara, "This is a great and important day."

Harlem's *Amsterdam News* reported, "The Supreme Court decision is the greatest victory for the Negro people since the Emancipation Proclamation."

In North Carolina, teenager Julius Chambers, who later became a director for the Fund, gathered his classmates and teachers to celebrate. "We assumed that *Brown* was self-executing," he said. "The law had been announced and people would have to obey it. Wasn't that how things worked in America, even in White America?"

But on June 25, Governor Stanley

announced, "I shall use every legal means at my command to continue segregated schools in Virginia."

Marshall told reporters that if any state didn't obey the ruling, the NAACP would gladly take them back to court. "If they try it in the morning, we'll have them in court the next morning—or possibly that same afternoon."

"I'm in a hurry," he declared. "I want to put myself out of business. I want to get things to a point where there won't be an NAACP—just a National Association for the Advancement of People."

In June, at the NAACP's forty-fifth annual convention, Marshall told the crowd that schools should be desegregated "in no event, later than September of 1955."

During the summer some Southern communities began desegregating their schools. That fall in Baltimore, Maryland, nearly 3,000 black students were going to schools that had been all-white. The progress reports encouraged Marshall and his team.

In August, lawyer Lou Redding coached eleven black students as they

African American parents and children in Baltimore, Maryland, stand across the street from School No. 34 as white picketers march, nearly a month after classes had started with white and black pupils mingling peacefully. September 30, 1954 prepared to enter Milford High School in lower Delaware. "We were not smart enough to be afraid," recalled Orlando Camp, one of the students. "We felt it wouldn't be a big deal. We played with white kids in the summertime and we didn't feel intimidated."

Orlando had graduated from an all-black elementary school where they used books mimeographed from twenty-year-old books that were scribbled with pencil notes. "Getting an education in an all-white school would give us greater opportunities," he said. "My mother gave me one hundred and fifty dollars to get new clothes. This was a significant amount of money indeed for a poor black family. She was really happy."

"On the first day everything was calm," he remembered. There were three home-rooms and the black students were split up. "The teachers were courteous but not friendly." His biggest shock came when he opened the class's textbook: *Algebra II*! Orlando had never taken algebra before, and he needed tutoring to catch up.

That day, white kids went home and told their parents about their new black classmates. Phones began to ring. The next day, crowds gathered as Orlando and the other black students went to school. By the third day, a mob of two thousand angry white parents stood outside Milford High and called the black children names. They smashed lightbulbs on the street, making sounds like gunshots. Local police refused to protect the black students, so the state police drove the kids to school. Photographers and reporters showed up and dubbed the black students the Milford Eleven.

At that point a racist named Bryant Bowles, president of the National Association for the Advancement of White People, arrived in Milford from Baltimore and incited a near riot. He rallied to raise money for opposing integration. More than eight hundred white people signed a petition against desegregation, and the superintendent closed Milford High. After a cooling-off period, the state board of education ordered the school to be reopened. A new school board expelled Orlando and his ten schoolmates. Redding and Greenberg drew up a complaint and won a court order that the Milford Eleven be readmitted.

"We stuck it out," said Orlando. "We only had twenty-eight days in the white school. I wound up going to an all-black high school. But we made it possible for Milford to eventually integrate."

Similar demonstrations sprang up throughout the country. Marshall and the

Fund hired workers to advise the black community on how to go about seeking desegregation. Most black families wanted integration to begin as soon as possible.

The Supreme Court had set late October as a date for hearing a final round of arguments about how to implement their ruling. Marshall and his team prepared briefs for *Brown II*. Robinson, who had argued the Virginia case, urged Marshall to demand an order for immediate desegregation. Why make black children wait any longer for a good education? Other members of the team recommended a gradual approach, giving school boards a chance to make the transition. Marshall decided to adopt this strategy. The final brief offered school districts up to two years to completely integrate.

The Court postponed the date for the hearing. Finally, on April 11, 1955, Marshall appeared before the Supreme Court to argue *Brown II*. His old opponent, John W. Davis, had died. New attorneys represented South Carolina and six other Southern states. Their briefs gave reasons for holding off integration: "withdrawal of white children from public schools, racial tensions, violence, loss of jobs for black teachers. Virginia argued that blacks

Louis J. Redding (on the left) of Wilmington, Delaware, and Thurgood Marshall confer at the Supreme Court during a recess in the court's hearing on racial integration in the public schools. April 1955

scored far lower on IQ tests than whites," recorded Greenberg.

S. Emory Rogers, speaking on behalf of Clarendon County, said that the court's decision had presented his community with "terrific problems." Local attitudes would have to change slowly. "I do not believe," said Rogers, "that in a biracial society we can push the clock forward abruptly to 2015 or 2045. I do not think that...the white people of the district will send their children to the Negro schools."

Attorney I. Beverly Lake, representing North Carolina, blamed the court for outlawing segregation. He said that if the court ordered immediate integration it would be "a death blow [to public education]."

Attorney General John Ben Sheppered of Texas said, "Texas loves its Negro people. It is our problem—let us solve it."

On the fourth and final day, Marshall rebutted his opponents' arguments. "The very people...that would object to sending their white children to school with Negroes are eating food that has been prepared, served and almost put in their mouths by the mothers of those children."

Marshall wound up by saying all he asked for was equality. Black children would be expected to compete with white children without any special consideration. Teachers would be free to put "dumb colored children with dumb white children and smart colored children with smart white children." In closing, he asked the Court to set a deadline of September 1956 for complete integration.

On May 31, 1955, the Court unanimously ruled against setting deadlines. However, school districts would have to start making plans to enforce integration. Local federal judges would ensure that schools desegregate "with *all deliberate speed*."

Marshall wondered what that last phrase meant. Back in his NAACP office he griped about the decision to his lawyers. A secretary looked up "deliberate" in the dictionary. "The first word of similarity for *deliberate* is slow," she said. "Which means 'slow speed.'"

Marshall said, "Integration hasn't happened yet, that's how slow 'deliberate speed' is." Yet he knew they had won their case. The Court remained committed to ending school segregation. "It will not take a hundred years," he said, "that I can guarantee."

Baltimore Afro-American editorial page cartoon, ". . . With All Deliberate Speed," July 2, 1955. Publisher Carl Murphy felt that the ruling was a win for Marshall since the Court adhered to its plan to end school segregation in the United States.

EPILOGUE:
THE FIGHT GOES ON

MARSHALL said, "Unless our children begin to learn together, there is little hope that our people will ever learn to live together."

But many school systems stalled or refused to integrate. Greenberg described the resistance as "the backlash against our victory."

In August 1956, the Virginia legislature voted to defeat the desegregation law. They passed a law requiring the governor to close any public school threatened with integration. As a result, Governor J. Lindsay Almond, Jr., closed schools in Richmond, Charlottesville, Norfolk and Prince Edward County where Barbara Johns had led the student strike. The schools remained closed from 1959 to 1964.

In 1956, a few black students had enrolled in public schools in Sturgis and Clay, Kentucky. On the first day of school a mob of angry whites taunted them. Another mob chased photographers and reporters out of town. The governor, A. B. "Happy" Chandler, called out the National Guard and tanks arrived. Thousands of whites boycotted the school, and the black students were expelled.

Marshall assigned Greenberg and James Crumlin, a local black lawyer, to file cases and get the children back in school.

In Little Rock, Arkansas, the school board had approved a desegregation plan that would start in 1957. Three hundred black children were going to be enrolled in white schools. The school board decreased the number to seventy-five, then twenty-five. On September 2, 1957, the day before school was supposed to open, Governor Orval Faubus went on television and radio and announced that he had called out the National Guard to stop black children from entering Central High School. He warned that if black students were admitted, "Blood will run in the streets."

The parents of only nine teenagers agreed to let them risk entering the school. Each day the Little Rock Nine, as they were called, were escorted to Central High by troops of the 101st Airborne Division of the United States Army.

"During that school year," wrote Greenberg, "Thurgood, Connie Motley (a Fund lawyer), and I shuttled between New York and Little Rock, taking depositions, gathering facts, preparing further proceedings." On May 27, 1958, Ernest Green, one of the nine, became the first black to graduate from Central High.

Elizabeth Eckford at Little Rock Central High School, Little Rock, Arkansas, as troops block Negro students. September 1957.

Hazel Bryan Massery, one of the women behind Eckford, eventually apologized to her for trying to keep her from attending the all-white high school.

Top: Ernest Green, the first African American graduate of Little Rock Central High School, and his parents are escorted to a taxi following graduation ceremonies. Little Rock, Arkansas, 1958

Left: Left to right: Harry Briggs, Jr., Linda Brown Smith, Spottswood Thomas Bolling, Jr. and Ethel Louise Belton Brown, during a press conference celebrating the tenth anniversary of *Brown v. Board of Education.* May 1964

By the end of the 1950s, the Fund had gone back to court with sixty elementary and high school cases. "It was a struggle every inch of the way," said Greenberg. Forty years later he wrote, "What had all our efforts achieved?"

"The Brown decision...broke the silence," said Cheryl Brown Henderson, Linda's younger sister. "It made the country start talking about racism and segrega-tion and discrimination and second-class citizenship."

Linda Brown Thompson said, "I think if we had to do it all over again, we would certainly not hesitate because it made so much of a difference in the world around us and...here in the United States. That case has impacted and touched someone in every facet of life."

John Watson, one of the plaintiffs in Prince Edward County, said, "Every ten years those of us who were involved in the five cases are invited to the White House." In 2014, President Obama greeted them and their families. "He stood there and shook hands with every one of us," remembered John.

"He gave all the ladies a little kiss on the cheek," recalled Joan Johns Cobb.

At the 60th anniversary celebration, President Obama proclaimed, "Today, the hope and promise of Brown remains unfulfilled. In the years to come, we must continue striving toward equal opportunities for all our children…Because when

Joan and Claude Cobbs with President Barack Obama at the White House celebrating the sixtieth anniversary of *Brown v. Board of Education.* May 17, 2014

children learn and play together, they grow, build, and thrive together."

Where are we today with integrating schools?

"I had thought, we all thought, that once we got the Brown case, the thing was going to be over," said Thurgood Marshall. "You see, we were always looking for that one case to end all of it [segregation in schools]. And that case hasn't come up yet."

In 1974, the Supreme Court heard a lawsuit called *Millikin v. Bradley* that involved schools in Detroit. By then Marshall was a Supreme Court justice, having been nominated by President Lyndon Johnson in 1967, and he heard the case.

The NAACP on behalf of black parents had sued Governor William Milliken of Michigan to introduce busing as a method for integrating public schools. Black children would be bused into the suburbs, and white children from fifty-three districts would be bused into the city. Detroit's black population had grown overwhelmingly, and many white families had fled to the suburbs so that their children could attend all-white schools. The black parents won in the lower court and appeals court. However, the Supreme Court overturned the rul-

ing and decided that school districts were not obligated to desegregate. The plan for busing was "wholly impermissible," they ruled, and therefore unconstitutional.

Justice Marshall disagreed and read his dissenting opinion aloud. Referring to *Brown v. Board of Education*, he said, "This court held that segregation of children in public schools on the basis of race deprives Negro children of equal educational opportunities and therefore denies them the equal protection of the laws.... We deal here with the rights of all our children, whatever their race, to an equal start in life. Those children who have been denied that right in the past deserve better than to see fences thrown up to deny them that right in the future." In closing he said, "After twenty years of small, often difficult steps toward that great end [of school segregation], the court today takes a giant step backwards."

The Court's ruling in *Millikin v. Bradley* set a trend toward resegregating schools. Over the next two decades Detroit's public schools became almost entirely black. The case impacted other parts of the country as well: Boston, Massachusetts; Cleveland, Ohio; Kansas City, Kansas and Pasadena, California.

"Busing became a national issue,"

Girls in integrated classroom, Anacostia High School, Washington, D.C.

wrote Greenberg. The subject caused heated debates, fights and even riots. Those in favor of busing saw it as an affordable way to achieve school integration and create a more tolerant society. Those against it objected to having their children take long rides to and from school. Wasn't this Oliver Brown's argument back in 1950 when his daughter Linda rode the bus to Monroe? Once again, parents demanded that their children go to neighborhood schools.

Meanwhile, in the 1990s, the courts relaxed their supervision of school dis-tricts' efforts to integrate. They casu-ally applied the phrase "with all deliberate speed" from *Brown II* and practically ignored steps toward integra-tion. "There are clear signs that progress is coming undone and that the nation is headed backwards toward greater segre-gation of black students," stated a Civil Rights Project from Harvard University in 1997. "Segregation is spreading across the nation."

A federal judge in Tuscaloosa, Okla-homa, freed city schools from the order to desegregate. "In Tuscaloosa today," said

Nikole Hannah-Jones on *Pro Publica*, "nearly one in three black students attends a school that looks as if *Brown v. Board of Education* never happened."

"Are we losing the Dream?" asked the Harvard Civil Rights project in 2003. "Resegregation is happening."

In 2014, Richard Rothstein reported in the *Washington Post*, "Schools remain segregated today because neighborhoods in which they are located are segregated. Today things are getting worse."

But the Harvard project concluded that most Americans believe in desegregation, and "more, not less, should be done to increase integrated education." They suggested that private schools develop plans to diversify, and that poor minority families could move to suburban communities with better schools.

The Southern Poverty Law Center (SPLC), based in Montgomery, Alabama, strives to change attitudes with a program called Teaching Tolerance. They produce films, books and newsletters. The SPLC claims that students in integrated schools perform better on tests and are more likely to go to college and hold good jobs.

Orlando Camp, one of the eleven students who integrated Milford High in Delaware in 1954, took part in dedicating a historical plaque to mark the fifty-year anniversary. Eighth graders at Milford listened to his story and bombarded him with questions about the Jim Crow era. Devon Shiels said it made him think "how society has changed."

Cassy Galon and J'Quanna Stratford agreed but said, "It still happens today; it's better in schools today but some parents don't teach their kids that racism is wrong."

"Change doesn't come easy to a small town," wrote Camp. On receiving an honorary diploma that "healed old wounds," he said, "In a small way this is a personal legacy for my children and grandkids to never give up, don't quit, follow your dreams—they can come true."

Marshall realized that despite the victory in *Brown v. Board of Education*, he and his colleagues had not achieved their goal. He recalled the words of his mentor, Charles Houston, who had started fighting with him in 1935 to end segregation in schools. "Do not lose heart if victory does not come at once," Houston had said to Marshall and the NAACP Legal Defense Fund attorneys. "Persevere to the end."

Negro Schoolhouse near Summerville, South Carolina, by Marion Post Walcott

TIMELINE

1839: A songbook published in Ithaca, New York, ridicules a minstrel show character named Jim Crow. The term came to be used as a racial slur.

1849: Benjamin F. Roberts, a black man in Boston, tries to enroll his daughter Sarah in a school for whites. The Massachusetts school board turns him down. He takes his case to court and the judge rules that segregation is legal.

1863: President Abraham Lincoln issues the Emancipation Proclamation during the Civil War declaring that all persons held as slaves within the rebellious states shall be free.

1866: The Civil Rights Act of 1866 guarantees blacks basic economic rights.

1868: The Fourteenth Amendment to the Constitution is ratified. It guarantees that all persons born or naturalized in the United States are citizens of the United States, and that no state shall deprive any person of life, liberty or property without due process of law, or deny to any person the equal protection of the law.

1869: Louisiana passes a law forbidding segregation in public transportation.

1875: The Civil Rights Act of 1875 is passed by Congress. It prohibits discrimination in inns, theaters and other public places. Public schools, a relatively new institution, are not included.

1877: The Louisiana law of 1869 is overturned by the Supreme Court in *Hall v. DeCuir*.

1883: The Supreme Court overturns the Civil Rights Act of 1875 and declares that the Fourteenth Amendment does not prohibit discrimination by private individuals or businesses.

1887: The practices of racial segregation known as Jim Crow begin. Florida passes the first railway segregation act, followed by Mississippi, then Texas.

1890: The Louisiana legislature passes a law requiring railroads to provide separate but equal passenger coaches for white and colored races.

1892: Homer A. Plessy, a black man, challenges the law by sitting in a Louisiana railroad car reserved for whites. Plessy is arrested and goes to court in New Orleans. He argues that the segregation law violates the Fourteenth Amendment, but the judge rules against him.

1896: The United States Supreme Court hands down its decision in *Plessy v. Ferguson*. Separate but equal facilities for white and black railroad passengers do not violate the Equal Protection Clause of the Fourteenth Amendment.

1908: Thoroughgood Marshall is born in Baltimore, Maryland, on July 2. At age six he shortens his first name to Thurgood.

1909: The National Association for the Advancement of Colored People (NAACP) is founded. Headquarters are based in New York City.

1912: A branch of the NAACP opens in Baltimore. In Washington, D.C., President Woodrow Wilson segregates government offices and fires or demotes many blacks in government jobs.

1925: Thurgood Marshall enters Lincoln University with the goal of becoming a lawyer.

1927: In the case *Gong Lum v. Rice*, the Supreme Court rules that a Mississippi school district may require a Chinese American girl to attend a segregated black school instead of a school for whites.

1929: Charles Hamilton Houston becomes dean of Howard University Law School in Washington, D.C., a law school for blacks.

1930: Marshall enrolls at Howard University Law School, and Dean Charles Houston becomes his role model and mentor.

1933: Marshall opens a law practice in Baltimore. He takes fact-finding trips with Charles Houston for the NAACP.

1935: Marshall helps Houston win *Murray v. Pearson*, his first civil rights case, desegregating the University of Maryland Law School.

1936: Marshall signs a six-month contract with the NAACP and moves to New York City.

1938: On November 9, Houston and Marshall defend Lloyd Gaines in *State of Missouri ex rel. Gaines v. Canada*. The United States Supreme Court decides in favor of Lloyd Gaines, a black student who had been refused admission to the University of Missouri Law School.

1939: Thurgood Marshall is named special counsel of the NAACP.

1940: Marshall serves as legal director of the NAACP from 1940 till 1961.

1944: In Westminster, California, Sylvia Mendez and her younger brothers try to enroll in public school but are refused admittance because of their dark skin and Mexican last name. Their father, Gonzalo Mendez, sues the school district and the case goes to trial. On March 18, 1946, Judge Paul J. McCormick rules in favor of the Mendez family, and in 1947, the Ninth Circuit Court of Appeals in San Francisco unanimously upholds the ruling.

1948: January. *Sipuel v. Board of Regents of University of Oklahoma*. Ada Lois Sipuel is denied entrance to the all-white University of Oklahoma Law School because of her race. Marshall argues Sipuel's case before the United States Supreme Court, which rules in favor of Sipuel. The Oklahoma state board of regents then creates a new law school for blacks in the state capitol building. Marshall goes back to court to prove that the Jim Crow law school is inferior, but the University of Oklahoma admits Sipuel and makes her sit in back of the classroom.

1948: The NAACP board of directors formally endorses Marshall's view on segregation strategy: an all-out attack on segregation in education.

1949: *Briggs et al. v. Elliott et al.* Marshall and NAACP officials meet with black residents of Clarendon County, South Carolina. They decide to launch a test case against segregation in public schools if at least twenty plaintiffs can be found. Harry Briggs and nineteen other parents sign the petition, and the NAACP files a class action lawsuit against the Clarendon County School Board.

1950: On April 4, in *Sweatt v. Painter* Marshall defends Herman Marion Sweatt, a black mailman who applied for admission to the University of Texas

Law School in 1946 but was rejected solely because of his race. Marshall appeals to the United States Supreme Court and argues that Sweatt has a constitutional right to attend the law school. The Court decides in his favor, and Sweatt is ordered to be admitted to the University of Texas Law School.

1950: In December *Bolling v. Sharpe* is argued. Gardner Bishop, a black barber in Washington, D.C., tries to enroll a group of black students at the new all-white John Philip Sousa Junior High School, but they are turned away. Charles Houston represents Bishop and the students, one of whom is named Spottswood Bolling, Jr. Houston suffers a heart attack, and his colleague James Madison Nabrit, Jr., takes over and in 1951 files a lawsuit against the Board of Education of the District of Columbia. The case becomes part of *Brown v. Board of Education.*

1951: In June *Brown v. Board of Education* is argued in the U.S. District Court for Kansas. In Topeka, Kansas, Oliver Brown attempts to enroll his daughter Linda Carol, a third grader, in the all-white elementary school in their neighborhood. But she is refused admittance because lower grades in Topeka are segregated. Oliver Brown and twelve other black parents file a lawsuit against the Topeka Board of Education. Marshall's top assistant, Robert Carter, leads the NAACP legal team into trial. In August 1951, a three-judge panel at the United States District Court holds that "no willful, intentional or substantial discrimination" exists in Topeka's schools. In October, the NAACP lawyers appeal the case to the United States Supreme Court.

1951: On April 23, Barbara Rose Johns, a sixteen-year-old junior at Robert R. Moton High School in Farmville, Virginia, leads the entire student body on a strike to protest conditions. NAACP lawyers Spottswood Robinson III and Oliver Hill file a lawsuit on behalf of the students. The case is titled *Davis et al. v. County School Board of Prince Edward County, Virginia, et al.*

1951: In October *Belton v. Gebhart* is argued in Delaware with *Bulah v. Gebhart.* Ethel Louise Belton can't attend the all-white high school in the suburb of Clayton, Delaware, where she lives. Instead, she has to travel ten miles to an inferior black high school in downtown Wilmington. Her mother and a group of other black parents ask Louise Lorenzo Redding to file a suit against Francis B. Gebhart, the school board president for their county.

1951: In October *Bulah v. Gebhart* is argued. Mrs. Fred Bulah's eight-year-old daughter, Shirley Barbara, is not permitted to take a bus for white children to the one-room schoolhouse in Hockessin, Delaware, so Louis Lorenzo Redding files a lawsuit in Wilmington. The two Delaware cases go to trial on October 22, 1951.

1952: On April 1, Chancellor Collins J. Seitz rules in favor of the plaintiffs in the Delaware cases and orders that all of the children are to be immediately admitted to white schools. Delaware's attorney general appeals the decision.

1952: On April 23, *Davis v. County School Board of Prince Edward County* goes to trial in Richmond, Virginia. The court rules in favor of the school board under the theory of "separate but equal." Thurgood Marshall appeals the decision.

1952: June. The Supreme Court announces that it will hear oral arguments in *Briggs* and *Brown* during the upcoming October term. The Court announces a postponement, then says it will also hear the Delaware cases, as well as *Davis v. Prince Edward County* and *Bolling et al. v. Sharpe et al.*

1952: December 9–11. The first round of argument is held in *Brown* and its companion cases.

1953: On September 8, Chief Justice Fred Vinson dies. President Dwight D. Eisenhower nominates California Governor Earl Warren to replace Vinson as interim chief. The Court reschedules arguments in *Brown* for December.

1953: In October the Supreme Court orders that a second round of arguments in *Brown v. Board* be heard.

1953: From December 7–9, a second round of arguments in *Brown v. Board of Education* is heard.

1954: On March 1, the Senate confirms Earl Warren as Chief Justice.

1954: On May 17, the Court overturns *Plessy v. Ferguson* and declares that racial segregation in public schools violates the Equal Protection clause of the Fourteenth Amendment. That same day the Court holds that racial segregation in the District of Columbia public schools violates the Due Process Clause of the Fifth Amendment in *Bolling v. Sharpe*. The Court schedules arguments on means for putting the ruling into effect for October, but postpones until April of 1955.

1954: May. Barbara Rose Johns's family's house in Darlington Heights, Virginia, is burned down in retaliation for the Supreme Court ruling.

1954: June. Governor Stanley of Virginia announces he will use every legal means to continue segregated schools.

1954: On September 8, Orlando Camp and ten other black students attend the all-white Milford High School in lower Delaware. On September 17, a mass meeting of whites is held and a petition is signed to remove the black students known as the Milford Eleven. Milford High is closed. Racist Bryant Bowles arrives, and a new school board expells Orlando and his ten classmates.

1955: April. The Supreme Court hears its third round of arguments in *Brown*, this time concerning remedies. On May 31, the Supreme Court hands down *Brown II*, ordering that desegregation occur with "all deliberate speed."

1956: The Virginia legislature votes to defeat the desegregation law. Public schools in Richmond, Charlottesville, Norfolk and Prince Edward County are closed from 1959 to 1964.

1957: In September in Little Rock, Arkansas, nine black teenagers escorted by United States army troops enter the all-white Central High School despite threats from Governor Orval Faubus. The students are known as the Little Rock Nine.

1964: The plaintiffs involved in the five cases known as *Brown v. Board of Education* attend an anniversary celebration at the White House in Washington, D.C., and a celebration continues to be held every ten years.

1967: Thurgood Marshall becomes the first African American appointed to the United States Supreme Court and serves until 1991, when he retires.

BRIEF SUMMARIES OF THE CASES

Plessy v. Ferguson

In 1869, Louisiana passed a law *forbidding* segregation in public transportation, but the law was overturned by the United States Supreme Court in 1877. By 1892, eight states, including Louisiana, had laws segregating railroad cars, streetcars and riverboats.

The blacks of Louisiana tested the law. On June 7, 1892, a light-skinned black man named Homer Adolph Plessy boarded a train in New Orleans and sat in a car reserved for whites. A conductor asked him to move into the car for "colored passengers," but Plessy refused and was arrested. At trial in New Orleans, Plessy argued that the segregation law in Louisiana violated the Fourteenth Amendment, which guarantees equal rights to all citizens of the United States. The court ruled against him. He appealed to the Louisiana Supreme Court and lost. He then appealed to the Supreme Court of the United States. In 1896, the Court handed down its opinion: The practice of segregation in Louisiana did not violate the Fourteenth Amendment. Racially separate facilities were legal as long as they were equal. "Separate but equal" became the law of the land.

Gonzalo Mendez et al. v. Westminster School District of Orange County et al.

In 1944, Sylvia Mendez, a nine-year-old girl of Mexican descent, and her younger brothers Gonzalo Jr. and Jerome, tried to enroll in public school in Westminster, California. School officials refused to admit them because of their dark skin and Mexican last name, and sent the children to a school for Mexican Americans in another district. Their father, Gonzalo Mendez, a naturalized citizen, sued the Westminster school district. His lawyer enlarged the case to include five Latino families, and they sued four school districts. On March 18, 1946, Judge Paul J.

McCormick ruled in favor of the Mendez family. Segregation in California public schools created "antagonisms in the children" and "violated the equal protection clause." The school district appealed the decision, but on April 15, 1947, the Ninth Circuit Court of Appeals in San Francisco unanimously upheld the ruling.

Sweatt v. Painter

Herman Marion Sweatt, a black postman and veteran of World War II, applied to Texas State University Law School in 1946, but was rejected because of his race. Sweatt filed a lawsuit with help from the NAACP. At that time there was no law school for blacks in Texas. The court gave Texas six months to establish one at a vocational school. When the case was heard by the state Court of Civil Appeals, the legislature approved money for building a better law school for blacks in an office building in Austin. The school consisted of three rooms in the basement. Classes began in March 1947, but Sweatt refused to enroll. He went back to court, defended by Thurgood Marshall and members of the NAACP Legal Defense Fund. The court ruled against Sweatt. In 1948, Marshall appealed the ruling and lost again. Finally, he took the case to the Supreme Court of the United States. Marshall argued that Sweatt had a constitutional right to attend the state law school. In June 1950, the Court held unanimously that the new law school for blacks did not offer an equal education. Sweatt was ordered to be admitted to the Texas University Law School.

Brown v. Board of Education of Topeka

In fall 1950, Oliver Brown attempted to enroll his daughter Linda Carol, a third grader, in the neighborhood elementary school. The principal refused to accept Linda at the all-white school. Elementary schools in Topeka, Kansas, were legally segregated. So her father and twelve other black parents filed suit against the Topeka Board of Education on behalf of their children. Under the leadership of the NAACP, they wanted to end segregation in public schools. The case went to trial in Topeka's federal court in June 1951. Thurgood Marshall's assistants Robert Carter and Jack Greenberg represented Brown. In August, the court ruled unanimously against Brown and the other plaintiffs. Marshall still saw this school case as an excellent opportunity to challenge segregation laws. On

October 1, 1951, the NAACP lawyers appealed the case to the Supreme Court of the United States. By December 1952, the Court combined the case with four similar cases from Delaware, South Carolina, Virginia and Washington, D.C. *Brown* was second on the list but happened to be moved to the top, so all five cases were known as *Brown v. Board of Education*.

Briggs v. Elliott

Black children in Clarendon County, South Carolina, had no buses to take them to schools, which were wooden shacks without running water or flushing toilets. In 1947, a group of angry parents led by Levi Pearson and Reverend Joseph Albert DeLaine sued local officials for bus service. The case was thrown out of court on a technicality, but Pearson, DeLaine and members of the NAACP asked Thurgood Marshall to help file a new lawsuit. Now they demanded better schools, equal to those of the whites. Marshall said he would take the case if they could find twenty plaintiffs willing to risk fighting for school integration. DeLaine found the plaintiffs and listed their names alphabetically, starting with Harry Briggs. So the case was called *Briggs v. Elliott*. Elliott was the chairman of School District 22, where all the children named in the lawsuit attended school. The case went to trial on May 28, 1951, in the federal court in Charleston, South Carolina. Three weeks later, the court denied the plaintiffs' plea. But they ordered the defendants to "promptly" start improving conditions for black children. Marshall appealed the case to the Supreme Court of the United States, and it became one of the five cases grouped for argument as *Brown v. Board of Education*.

Davis v. County School Board of Prince Edward County

Barbara Rose Johns, a sixteen-year-old junior at Robert R. Moton High School in Prince Edward County, Virginia, organized a student walkout to protest conditions. Moton, a school for blacks, had no gym, cafeteria or auditorium with fixed seats. Wooden shacks covered with tar paper had been added as relief for overcrowded classrooms. Although the white school board kept promising to make improvements, nothing happened. On April 23, 1951, Barbara led the entire student body on strike. She and her coleaders wrote to the NAACP lawyers for their region and asked for help. Lawyers Oliver Hill and Spottswood

Robinson III arrived and said the NAACP would become involved if the students sued for the end of segregation. The students approved and Robinson filed a suit on their behalf. The first person who signed the petition was Dorothy E. Davis, a ninth grader, so the case was titled *Davis v. County School Board of Prince Edward County.*

The trial began at the federal courthouse in Richmond, Virginia, on February 25, 1952. The court ruled against the students of Moton and said that segregated schools were part of Southern tradition. However, the judges agreed that the high school for black children was unequal to the high school for whites, and they ordered the Prince Edward school board to quickly equalize school buildings, curriculum and transportation. Thurgood Marshall appealed the decision, and the case was heard by the Supreme Court as part of *Brown v. Board of Education.*

Bulah v. Gebhart and Belton v. Gebhart

Ethel Louise Belton, a tenth grader, suffered from a cardiac condition, yet she traveled ninety minutes to a black high school in Wilmington, Delaware. She lived in the suburb of Clayton but couldn't go to the all-white school in her community. In March 1951, she and her mother and a group of black parents from Clayton met with Louis Lorenzo Redding, Delaware's first black lawyer. Redding advised the parents to ask the State Board of Education to admit their children to the local white high school. The parents tried without success, so Ethel and nine other plaintiffs filed a suit against Francis B. Gebhart, the school board president for their county.

Meanwhile, in Hockessin, Delaware, the mother of eight-year-old Shirley Barbara Bulah had to drive her daughter to a one-room schoolhouse. A bus for white children passed their front door every day. Mrs. Bulah wrote letters to state officials, and even the governor, requesting permission for Shirley to ride the bus. Finally, she was told that Delaware required separate schools for black and white children, and Shirley could not ride a bus serving a white school. Louis Redding filed a lawsuit for the Bulahs in Wilmington.

Chancellor Collins J. Seitz presided over the Court of Chancery to hear the two cases, *Belton v. Gebhart* and *Bulah v. Gebhart*. The trial began on October 22, 1951. Jack Greenberg, a member of Marshall's staff, assisted Redding. Chancellor Seitz visited the schools that Ethel and Shirley attended. Five months later he issued his opinion in favor of the plaintiffs and ordered that all of them to be immediately enrolled at the white schools in their communities. Delaware's Attorney General, Albert Young, appealed the decision, but the Delaware Supreme Court upheld Seitz's ruling. Young filed an appeal with the United States Supreme Court. *Francis B. Gebhart, et al. v. Ethel Louise Belton et al.* was added to *Brown v. Board of Education of Topeka*.

Bolling v. Sharpe

By 1947, public schools for blacks in Washington, D.C., were overcrowded and held shortened double and triple sessions. Gardner Bishop, a barber, was furious that his daughter attended school part-time, and he formed a parent protest group, that demand that half-empty white schools be turned over to them.

In 1948, Bishop began working with NAACP lawyer Charles Houston, who filed lawsuits to win equal schools for black children in Washington. Houston suffered a heart attack and referred Bishop to his colleague, James Madison Nabrit, Jr., a professor of law. Nabrit accepted the case on condition that Bishop gather plaintiffs to sue against school segregation itself. On September 11, 1950, Bishop led eleven black children to the new all-white John Philip Sousa Junior High School and asked the principal to enroll them. The principal refused, so the children sued to be admitted. One of the students was twelve-year-old Spottswood Thomas Bolling, Jr., and his name headed the list of plaintiffs. In 1951, Nabrit filed a suit against C. Melvin Sharpe, president of the Board of Education of the District of Columbia, and the case was titled *Bolling et al. v. Sharpe*. Nabrit brought his case to the United States District Court, but the judge threw the case out. As Nabrit prepared to appeal his case he received a call from a clerk at the Supreme Court: Chief Justice Fred M. Vinson wanted Nabrit's case to be decided with Marshall's school cases as part of *Brown v. Board of Education*.

TEXT OF THE FOURTEENTH AMENDMENT

Section 1. All persons born or naturalized in the United States, and subject to the jurisdiction thereof, are citizens of the United States and of the State wherein they reside. No State shall make or enforce any law which shall abridge the privileges or immunities of citizens of the United States; nor shall any State deprive any person of life, liberty, or property, without due process of law; nor deny to any person within its jurisdiction the equal protection of the laws.

Section 2. Representatives shall be apportioned among the several States according to their respective numbers, counting the whole number of persons in each State, excluding Indians not taxed. But when the right to vote at any election for the choice of electors for President and Vice President of the United States, Representatives in Congress, the Executive and Judicial officers of a State, or the members of the Legislature thereof, is denied to any of the male inhabitants of such State, being twenty-one years of age, and citizens of the United States, or in any way abridged, except for participation in rebellion, or other crime, the basis of representation therein shall be reduced in the proportion which the number of such male citizens shall bear to the whole number of male citizens twenty-one years of age in such State.

Section 3. No person shall be a Senator or Representative in Congress, or elector of President and Vice President, or hold any office, civil or military, under the United States, or under any State, who, having previously taken an oath, as a member of Congress, or as an officer of the United States, or as a member of any State legislature, or as an executive or judicial officer of any State, to support the

Constitution of the United States, shall have engaged in insurrection or rebellion against the same, or given aid or comfort to the enemies thereof. But Congress may by a vote of two-thirds of each House, remove such disability.

Section 4. The validity of the public debt of the United States, authorized by law, including debts incurred for payment of pensions and bounties for services in suppressing insurrection or rebellion, shall not be questioned. But neither the United States nor any State shall assume or pay any debt or obligation incurred in aid of insurrection or rebellion against the United States, or any claim for the loss or emancipation of any slave; but all such debts, obligations and claims shall be held illegal and void.

Section 5. The Congress shall have power to enforce, by appropriate legislation, the provisions of this article.

TEXT OF BROWN V. BOARD OF EDUCATION OF TOPEKA

May 17, 1954

Mr. Chief Justice Warren delivered the opinion of the court.

These cases come to us from the state of Kansas, South Carolina, Virginia, and Delaware. They are premised on different facts and different local conditions, but a common legal question justifies their consideration together in this consolidated opinion.

In each of the cases, minors of the Negro race, through their legal representatives, seek the aid of the courts in obtaining admission to the public schools of their community on a nonsegregated basis. In each instance, they had been denied admission to schools attended by white children under laws requiring or permitting segregation according to race. This segregation was alleged to deprive the plaintiffs of the equal protection of the laws under the Fourteenth Amendment. In each of the cases other than the Delaware case, a three-judge federal district court denied relief to the plaintiffs on the so-called "separate but equal" doctrine announced by this court in Plessy v. Ferguson, 163 U.S. 537. Under that doctrine, equality of treatment is accorded when the races are provided substantially equal facilities, even though these facilities be separate. In the Delaware case, the Supreme Court of Delaware adhered to that doctrine, but ordered that the plaintiffs be admitted to the white schools because of their superiority to the Negro schools.

The plaintiffs contend that segregated public schools are not "equal" and cannot be made "equal," and that hence they are deprived of the equal protection of the laws. Because of the obvious importance of the question presented, the court took jurisdiction. Argument was heard in the 1952 term, and reargument was heard this term on certain questions propounded by the court.

Reargument was largely devoted to the circumstances surrounding the adoption of the Fourteenth Amendment in 1868. It covered exhaustively consideration of the amendment in Congress, ratification by the states, then existing practices in racial segregation, and the views of proponents and opponents of the amendment. This discussion and our own investigation convince us that, although these sources cast some light, it is not enough to resolve the problem with which we are faced. At best, they are inconclusive. The most avid proponents of the postwar amendments undoubtedly intended them to remove all legal distinctions among "all persons born or naturalized in the United States." Their opponents, just as certainly, were antagonistic to both the letter and the spirit of the amendments and wished them to have the most limited effect. What others in Congress and the state legislatures had in mind cannot be determined with any degree of certainty.

An additional reason for the inconclusive nature of the amendment's history, with respect to segregated schools, is the status of public education at that time. In the South, the movement toward free common schools, supported by general taxation, had not yet taken hold. Education of white children was largely in the hands of private groups. Education of Negroes was almost non-existent, and practically all of the race were illiterate. In fact, any education of Negroes was forbidden by law in some states. Today, in contrast, many Negroes have achieved outstanding success in the arts and sciences as well as in the business and professional world.

It is true that public school education at the time of the amendment had advanced further in the North, but the effect of the amendment on northern states was generally ignored in the Congressional debates. Even in the North, the conditions of public education did not approximate those existing today. The curriculum was usually rudimentary; ungraded schools were common in rural areas; the school term was but three months a year in many states; and compulsory school attendance was virtually unknown. As a consequence, it is not surprising that there should be so little in the history of the Fourteenth Amendment relating to its intended effect on public education.

In the first cases in this court construing the Fourteenth Amendment, decided shortly after its adoption, the court interpreted it as proscribing all state-imposed discriminations against the Negro race. The doctrine of "separate but equal" did not make its appearance in this court until 1896 in the case of Plessy v. Ferguson, supra, involving not education but transportation. American courts have since labored with the doctrine for over half a century. In this court, there have been six cases involving the "separate but equal" doctrine in the field of public education. In Cumming v. County Board of Education, 175 U.S. 528, the Gong Lum v. Rice, 275 U.S. 78, the validity of the doctrine itself was not challenged. In more recent cases, all on the graduate school level, inequality was found in that specific benefits enjoyed by white students were denied to Negro students of the same educational qualifications. Missouri ex rel. Gaines v. Canada, 305 U.S. 337; Sipuel v. Oklahoma, 332 U.S. 631; Sweatt v. Painter, 339 U.S. 629; McLaurin v. Oklahoma State Regents, 339 U.S. 637. In none of these cases was it necessary to re-examine the doctrine to grant relief to the Negro plaintiff. And in Sweatt v. Painter, supra, the court expressly reserved decision on the question whether Plessy v. Ferguson should be held inapplicable to public education.

In the instant cases, that question is directly presented. Here, unlike Sweatt v. Painter, there are findings below that the Negro and white schools involved have been equalized, or are being equalized, with respect to buildings, curricula, qualifications and salaries of teachers, and other "tangible" factors. Our decision, there-fore, cannot turn on merely a comparison of these tangible factors in the Negro and white schools involved in each of the cases. We must look instead to the effect of segregation itself on public education.

In approaching this problem, we cannot turn the clock back to 1868 when the amendment was adopted, or even to 1896 when Plessy v. Ferguson was written. We must consider public education in the light of its full development and its present place in American life throughout the nation. Only in this way can it be determined if segregation in public schools deprives these plaintiffs of the equal protection of the laws.

Today, education is perhaps the most important function of state and local gov-ernments. Compulsory school attendance laws and the great expenditures for education both demonstrate our recognition of the importance of education to our democratic society. It is required in the performance of our most basic public responsibilities, even service in the armed forces. It is the very foundation of good citizenship. Today it is a principal instrument in awakening the child to cultural values, in preparing him for later professional training, and in helping him to adjust normally to his environment. In these days, it is doubtful that any child may reasonably be expected to succeed in life if he is denied the opportunity of an education. Such an opportunity, where the state has undertaken to provide it, is a right which must be made available to all on equal terms.

We come then to the question presented: Does segregation of children in public schools solely on the basis of race, even though the physical facilities and other "tangible" factors may be equal, deprive the children of the minority group of equal educational opportunities? We believe that it does.

In Sweatt v. Painter, supra, in finding that a segregated law school for Negroes could not provide them equal educational opportunities, this court relied in large part on "those qualities which are incapable of objective measurement but which make for greatness in a law school." In McLaurin v. Oklahoma State Regents, supra, the court, in requiring that a Negro admitted to a white graduate school be treated like all other students, again resorted to intangible considerations: "...His ability to study, to engage in discussions and exchange views with other students, and, in general, to learn his profession." Such considerations apply with added force to children in grade and high schools. To separate them from others of similar age and qualifications solely because of their race generates a feeling of inferiority as to their status in the community that may affect their hearts and minds in a way unlikely ever to be undone. The effect of this separation on their educational opportunities was well stated by the finding in the Kansas case by a court which nevertheless felt compelled to rule against the Negro plaintiffs:

"Segregation of white and colored children in public schools has a detrimental effect upon the colored children. The impact is greater when it has the sanction of the law; for the policy of separating the races is usually interpreted as denoting the inferiority of the Negro group. A sense of inferiority affects the motivation of a child to learn. Segregation with the sanction of law, therefore, has a tendency to (retard) the educational and mental development of Negro children and to deprive them of some of the benefits they would receive in a racially integrated school system."

Whatever may have been the extent of psychological knowledge at the time of Plessy v. Ferguson, this finding is amply supported by modern authority. Any language in Plessy v. Ferguson contrary to this finding is rejected.

We conclude that in the field of public education the doctrine of "separate but equal" has no place. Separate educational facilities are inherently unequal. Therefore, we hold that the plaintiffs and others similarly situated for whom the actions have been brought are, by reason of the segregation complained of, deprived of the equal protection of the laws guaranteed by the Fourteenth Amendment. This disposition makes unnecessary any discussion whether such segregation also violates the due process clause of the Fourteenth Amendment.

Because these are class actions, because of the wide applicability of this decision, and because of the great variety of local conditions, the formulation of decrees in these cases presents problems of considerable complexity. On reargument, the consideration of appropriate relief was necessarily subordinated to the primary question—the constitutionality of segregation in public education. We have now announced that such segregation is a denial of the equal protection of the laws. In order that we may have the full assistance of the parties in formulating decrees, the cases will be restored to the docket, and the parties are requested to present further argument on questions 4 and 5 previously propounded by the court for the reargument this term. The Attorney General of the United States is again invited to participate. The Attorneys General of the states requiring or permitting segregation in public education will also be permitted to appear as amici curiae upon request to do so by September 15, 1954, and submission of briefs by October 1, 1954. It is so ordered.

BIBLIOGRAPHY

Books

Camp, Orlando J., and Ed Kee. *The Milford Eleven*. Wilmington, Delaware: Cedar Tree Books, 2013.

Greenberg, Jack. *Crusaders in the Courts*. New York: Twelve Tables Press, 2004.

Hinton, KaaVonia. *Brown v. Board of Education of Topeka, Kansas, 1954*. Hockessin, Delaware: Mitchell Lane Publishers, 2010.

James, Jr., Rawn. Root and Branch: *Charles Hamilton Houston, Thurgood Marshall, and the Struggle to End Segregation*. New York: Bloomsbury Press, 2010.

Kanefield, Teri. *The Girl from the Tar Paper School*. New York: Abrams, 2014.

Kluger, Richard. *Simple Justice*. New York: Vintage Books, 2004.

Martin, Waldo E., Jr. *Brown v. Board of Education: A Brief History with Documents*. Boston and New York: Bedford/St. Martin's, 1998.

Motley, Constance Baker. *Equal Justice Under Law*. New York: Farrar, Straus and Giroux, 1998.

Patterson, James T. *Brown v. Board of Education: A Civil Rights Milestone and Its Troubled Legacy*. New York: Oxford University Press, 2001.

Pratt, Robert A. *The Color of Their Skin: Education and Race in Richmond, Virginia, 1954–89*. Charlottesville: The University Press of Virginia, 1992.

Smith, Bob. *They Closed Their Schools: Prince Edward County, Virginia, 1951–1964*. Farmville, Virginia: Martha E. Forrester, Council of Women, 1996.

Stokes, John A., with Lois Wolfe, Ph.D. *Students on Strike: Jim Crow, Civil Rights, Brown, and Me*. Washington, D.C.: National Geographic Society, 2008.

Thomas, Joyce Carol, ed. *Linda Brown, You Are Not Alone: The Brown v. Board of Education Decision*. New York: Hyperion Books, 2003.

Tonatiuh, Duncan. *Separate Is Never Equal*. New York: Abrams, 2014.

Tushnet, Mark V., ed. *Thurgood Marshall: His Speeches, Writings, Arguments, Opinions, and Reminiscences*. Chicago: Lawrence Hill Books, 2001.

Williams, Juan. *Thurgood Marshall: American Revolutionary*. New York: Three Rivers Press, 1998.

Articles

Adams, Alvin. "Negroes Who Won School Suit Ten Years Ago: Five Pioneers Find Neither." *Jet*, vol. XXVI, no. 6, May 21, 1964.

Frankenberg, Erica, and Chungmei Lee and Gary Orfield. "A Multiracial Society with

Segregated Schools: Are We Losing the Dream?" *The Civil Rights Project,* Harvard University. January 2003.

Hartocollis, Anemona. "Fresh Fuel in a Long Academic Debate." *The New York Times,* December 22, 2015.

June-Friesen, Katy. "Massive Resistance in a Small Town." *Humanities,* September/October 2013, Volume 34, Number 5.

Levine, Sheen S., and David Stark. "Diversity Makes You Brighter." *The New York Times,* Wednesday, December 9, 2015.

Martin, Douglas. "Shirley B. Stamps Dies at 59; Won '54 Desegregation Case." *The New York Times,* June 4, 2003.

McIlwain, Bill, and Alf Goodykoontz. "Segregation Case Plaintiffs Differ On Ruling Desired." *Richmond Times-Dispatch,* Sunday, December 13, 1953.

Millikan, Mona. "Negroes to Mark Court Victory Tuesday Night: Ruling by High Tribunal Hailed by NAACP Leaders." *Topeka Journal,* May 17, 1954.

Orfield, Gary, and Mark D. Bachmeier, David R. James and Tamela Eide. "Deepening Segregation in American Public Schools." *Southern Changes,* Vol. 19, No. 2, 1997.

Orfield, Gary , and Erica Frankenberg, Jongyeon Ee and John Kuscera. "Brown at 60: Great Progress, a Long Retreat and an Uncertain Future." *Civil Rights Project/Proyecto Derechos Civiles,* May 2014 (revised version 5-15-14).

Schuessler, Jennifer. "A President's Legacy Gets Complicated." *The New York Times,* November 30, 2015.

Strauss, Valerie. "How, after 60 years, Brown v. Board of Education succeeded—and didn't." *Washington Post,* April 24, 2014.

Radio Broadcasts/Online Articles

Camp, Orlando, and Ed Kee. "The Milford Eleven." *Delaware Today.* July 2012.

Davis, Elizabeth A. "The March on John Philip Sousa: A Social Action Project." Civil Rights Teaching, *Washington Post.*

Friedman, Michael J. *Justice for All: The Legacy of Thurgood Marshall.* U.S. Department of State January 2007. Photos.state.gov/libraries/amgov/30145/publications-english/Thurgood_marshall.pdf.

Hannah-Jones, Nikola. "Segregation Now." ProPublica, April 16, 2014, 11 p.m.

"Separate Is Not Equal: Brown v. Board of Education," Smithsonian National Museum of American History.

Talley, Robin. "What Happened in Prince Edward County." Posted September 27, 2014.

The White House: Office of the Press Secretary. Presidential Proclamation—60th Anniversary of Brown v. Board of Education, May 15, 2014.

Zonkel, Phillip. "Righting a Wrong: Mendez v. Westminster brought an end to segregation in O.C. schools—and ultimately throughout the state and nation," *Press Telegram.*

Transcripts of Oral Histories

PBS Newshour, Brown v. Board of Education, May 12, 2004, at 12:00 am EDT, courtesy of the Brown Foundation.

Interview with Linda Brown Thompson on August 12, 1993. Kansas State Historical

Society. Brown v. Board of Education of
Topeka, Oral History Project.

Interview with Eliza Briggs on May 19, 1995.
Kansas State Historical Society.

Interview with Vivian M. Scales on October 30,
1991. Kansas State Historical Society.

Interview with Mrs. Leola Brown Montgomery
on November 15, 1991. Kansas State
Historical Society.

Interview with Carrie Stokes on March 23,
1995. Kansas State Historical Society.

Williams, Rev. J. Samuel. The Five Lawsuits:
"The NAACP Strategy." National Parks
Service Transcript of Programming.

Interviews by Phone with Author

Alexander, June Shagaloff, July 15, 2014; May 5,
2015.

Cobb, Joan Johns, October 6, 2015.

Watson, John, October 1, 2015.

E-mails to Author

Cobb, Joan Johns, October 5, 2015.

Henderson, Cheryl Brown, November 28, 2014.

Videos

"Conversation with Veteran Organizer June
Shagaloff." July 15, 2014. NAACP. Calvin
Fortenberry, Director of Communications.

Milford Live. "MHSS Students Hear History of
School Desegregation." Thursday, November
05, 2015.

Further Resources

The Library of Congress

National Archives

Smithsonian National Museum of American
History

Places to Visit

United States Supreme Court, Washington,
D.C.

Smithsonian National Museum of American
History, Washington, D.C.

The Robert Russa Moton Museum, Farmville,
Virginia

Brown v. Board of Education National
Historical Site, Monroe Elementary
School, Topeka, Kansas

Milford Museum, Milford, Delaware

The Thurgood Marshall Center, Washington,
D.C.

SOURCE NOTES

Introduction

p. 1. "The trip wasn't . . . call us names." Stokes, 18.

p. 2. "slipped into . . . other kids." Stokes, 8.

p. 2. "I was so. . .that night." Stokes, 22.

p. 2. "for colored boys . . . at night." Stokes, 9.

p. 2. "take cover . . . bushes and trees." Stokes, 7.

p. 2. " I pray to . . . home safe." Stokes, 13.

p. 3. "Jim Crow was . . . citizens." Stokes, 22.

p. 3. "gala picnic." Kluger, *Simple Justice*, 376.

p. 4. "knowing his or . . . beating, or worse." Stokes, 23.

p. 5. "colored passengers." Kluger, 72."

p. 5. "separate but equal." Williams, *Thurgood Marshall: American Revolutionary*, 22.

p. 5. "It was too . . . cut it." Williams, 26.

p. 6. "Everybody in my . . . about segregation," Tushnet, 424.

p. 6. "We used to . . . wouldn't fight back." Williams, 30.

p. 6. "If anybody called . . . fought 'em." Williams, 30.

p. 6. "Either win . . . then and there." Williams, 15.

p. 6. "Don't you push . . . Yes, sir." Williams, 16.

p. 7. "Before I left . . . thing by heart." Kluger, 177.

p. 7. "We'd argue . . . from my dad." Williams, 35–36.

p. 7. "What do . . . Lawyer." Williams, 39.

p. 7. "Dummies' Retreat." Tushnet, editor.

Thurgood Marshall: His Speeches, Writings, Arguments, Opinions, and Reminiscences. 272.

p. 8. "He was training . . . for their people." Tushnet, 273.

p. 8. "He would tell . . . got to do it." Tushnet, 273.

p. 8. "The lawyer was . . . purpose in life." Williams, 59.

Chapter 1

p. 9. "We are convinced . . . segregated system." Williams, 182.

p. 10. "We won the big one." Williams, 185.

p. 10. "Our Greatest Civil Liberties Lawyer." Williams, 192.

pp.10- 11. "tall, burly . . . set [for] himself." Williams, 193.

p. 11. "wipe out . . . school to kindergarten." Williams, 195.

p. 11. "antagonisms in the children." Williams, 197.

p. 11. "school cases." Greenberg, *Crusaders in the Courts*, 124.

Chapter 2

p. 13. "I was very . . . cross the streets." Mrs. Leola Brown Montgomery, Interview, Oral History project transcript, p. 37.

p. 13. "Many times . . . bus got there." Kluger, 410.

p. 14. "I had all . . . just thrilled." PBS *Newshour*

p. 14. "I could hear . . . all of my playmates." Linda Brown Thompson, PBS *Newshour*, May 12, 2004, transcript.

p. 15. "My mom and dad . . . with these playmates." Interview with Linda Brown Thompson, August 12, 1993, Kansas State Historical Society, Oral History Project.

p. 15. "She was a . . . a great deal." Kluger, 378.

p. 16. "Our friends . . . back to church." Linda Brown Thompson, Interview, August 12, 1993.

p. 16. "Why should . . . each day?" Kluger, 410.

p. 17. "At first . . . of the plaintiffs." Leola Montgomery, PBS *Newshour*, May 12, 2004.

p. 17. "He was one . . . acted upon." Mrs. Leola Brown Montgomery, Interview, November 15, 1991, Kansas State Historical Society, Oral History Project.

Chapter 3

p. 18. "Do you think . . . each their children?" Kluger, 393.

p. 18. "We had absolutely . . . those days." Kluger, 197.

p. 20. "colored hotel." Kluger, 401.

p. 20. "simply a question of law." Kluger, 405.

p. 21. "Sometimes when . . . Randolph." Kluger, 408.

p. 21. "Not hardly . . . Seven blocks." Kluger, 410.

p. 21. "Objection will be sustained." Kluger, 411.

p. 21. "I couldn't wait . . . bunch of crackpots." Kluger, 411.

pp. 21-22. "We didn't know . . . against their will." Kluger, 411.

p. 22. "They [the teachers] . . . come up together." Kluger, 412.

p. 22. "Fleming inspire . . . the judges." Greenberg, 136.

p. 23. "The Topeka . . . under segregation." Kluger, 413.

p. 23. "I knew what . . . contradiction in terms." Kluger, 421.

p. 23. "In some cases . . . be the opposite." Greenberg, 138.

p. 23. "doomed to failure." Kluger, 422.

p. 23. "We lost . . . of ultimate victory." Greenberg, 138.

Chapter 4

p. 26. "We ain't asking . . . South Carolina gets." Kluger, 24.

p. 26. "Parents must stand . . . community." Kluger, 21.

p. 27. "At that . . . physical violence." Williams, 199.

p. 27. "The white folks . . . of my children." Kluger, 23.

p. 27. "Is this the . . . wholesome atmosphere?" Kluger, 24.

p. 27. "The black people . . . to break out." Kluger, 25.

Chapter 5

p. 28. " "I thought it . . . on the record." Kluger, 316.

p. 28. "I know these . . . this one exactly?" Kluger, 328.

p. 29. "It's dangerous . . . over there." Kluger, 328.

p. 30. "Didn't I tell . . . something to you." Kluger, 330.

p. 30. "bad." Kluger, 330.

p. 30. "This doesn't . . . crayon to show." Kluger, 330.

p. 30. "Everyone knew . . . it was." Kluger, 347.

p. 30. "I never did . . . get a hearing." Kluger, 346.

p. 31. "inequalities." Kluger, 347.

p. 31. "a reasonable time." Kluger, 348.

p. 32. "earth toilets." Kluger, 350.

p. 32. "outofdoor." Kluger, 350.

p. 32. "toilets." Kluger, 350.

p. 32. "I felt good . . . all come out." Kluger, 351.

p. 32. "I have reached. . . Negro child." Kluger, 353.

p. 32. "These children . . . definitely harmed." Kluger, 354.

pp. 32-33. "How much . . . impossible to answer." Kluger, 360.

p. 33. "A child who . . . function well." Kluger, 362363.

p. 33. "I think . . . is the school." Kluger, 363.

p. 33. "lasting, not temporary injury." Kluger, 365.

p. 33. "We ain't asking . . . first place." Kluger, 365.

p. 33. "promptly." Kluger, 366.

p. 33. "Segregation in . . . must be eradicated." Kluger, 367.

Chapter 6

p. 36. "the man . . . bother me a lot." Kluger, 467.

pp. 36-37. "Some of . . . unfair it was." Kluger, 467.

p. 37. "told her . . . about it?" Kluger, 468.

p. 37. "She said . . . over the world." Kluger, 468.

p. 37. "sound like a Southern businessman." John Watson, interview with author.

p. 39. "WE ARE . . . NEW SCHOOL." June-Friesen, (Online Article)

p. 39. "We knew . . . turned down." Kluger, 470.

p. 39. "Gentlemen: . . . when you arrive." Kluger, 471.

p. 39. "Grandma, I . . . Stick with us." Kluger, 471-472.

p. 39. "She was . . . her clothes." Kluger, 454.

p. 40. "Barbara Johns . . . as we could." Kluger, 471.

p. 40. "The kids . . . their hearts." Williams, 206.

p. 40. "It seemed . . . Mr. Hill." Kluger, 477.

p. 40. "We didn't pick . . . to their rescue." Williams, 206.

p. 40. "She had . . . her herself." Kluger, 452.

Chapter 7

p. 41. "Our people. . . settle it all." Kluger, 488.

p. 41. "We all . . . and we, theirs." Kluger, 486.

pp. 42-43."That's exactly . . . I did not." Kluger, 491.

p. 43. "Segregation is . . . official insult." Kluger, 493.

pp. 44-45. "What kind of . . . of the Negro." Kluger, 494-495.

p. 45. "a symbol of some stigma." Kluger, 496.

p. 45. "of what it . . . in America." Kluger, 497.

p. 45. "to see . . . loyal Americans." Kluger, 497.

p. 45. "I think . . . skin color." Kluger, 499-500.

p. 46. "catastrophe" . . . "legislate custom." Kluger, 501.

p. 46. "We were . . . formidable reputation." Kluger, 504.

p. 46. "the principle of . . . American life." Kluger, 504.

p. 46. "the Negro student . . . mixed schools." Kluger, 505.

p. 46. "no harm . . . either race." Kluger, 509.

p. 46. "There was . . . Supreme Court." Kluger, 487.

Chapter 8

p. 47. "When he . . . something about it." Judine Bishop Johnson (Internet) *The Five Lawsuits:* "The NAACP Strategy."

p. 48. "upper-crust blacks." Kluger, 515.

p. 48. "We knew . . . the lawyers." Kluger, 515.

p. 48. "We were mad . . . everyone." Kluger, 515-516.

p. 48. "These are children . . . and why." Kluger, 516.

p. 49. "I'd like to help." Kluger, 517.

p. 49. "He wanted . . . terribly concerned." Kluger, 517.

p. 49. "Well, . . . a lawyer." Kluger, 517.

p. 49. "Nabrit was . . . know him." Kluger, 519.

p. 53. "We had nothing . . . on segregation." Kluger, 291.

Chapter 9

p. 54. "We felt . . . Southern one." Kluger, 542.

p. 55. "We passed . . . climbing hills." *Jet*, "The Unfinished Agenda of Brown v. Board of Education," May 21, 1964.

p. 55. "I've always . . . close to home." *Jet*, May 21, 1964.

p. 55. "Howard . . . cold and dark." *Jet*, May 21, 1964.

p. 55. "Even in . . . to enroll." *Jet*, May 21, 1964.

p. 55. "We are all . . . and embarrassed." *Separate Is Not Equal*, Smithsonian National Museum of American History.

p. 55. "the pretty . . . the hill." Kluger, 435.

p. 55. "transportation facilities" . . . "private allowance." Kluger, 436.

p. 57. "He said . . . he'd help." Kluger, 436.

p. 57-58. "I was . . . for the colored." Kluger, 436.

Chapter 10

p. 59. "Early in . . . a great crew." Greenberg, 144.

pp. 59-60. "the first time . . . big mistake." Greenberg, 144.

p. 60. "most expensive.. . the menu." Kluger, 443.

p. 60. "Three out of . . . of inferiority." Kluger, 440–441.

p. 60. "He captivated . . . had to say." Greenberg, 145.

p. 61. "I travel . . . blocks away." Kluger, 443.

p. 61. "When we . . . and laugh." Kluger, 443.

p. 61. "When you . . . so hard." Kluger, 443.

p. 61. "If I . . . normal [and] natural." Kluger, 443444.

p. 61. "The others . . . the Germans." Kluger, 444.

p. 61. "did not . . . dishwashers." Kluger, 444.

p. 61. "The boys . . . comic books." Kluger, 444.

p. 61. "Most of . . . minds of the children." Kluger, 445.

p. 62. "vastly superior." Kluger, 450.

p. 62. "No. 29 . . . also outstanding." Kluger, 448.

p. 62. "I believe . . . Negro children." Kluger, 450.

p. 62. "Lou Redding . . . to white schools." Greenberg, 160.

p. 62. "This is . . . high schools." Kluger, 450–451.

p. 62. "Now we . . . Supreme Court." Greenberg, 161.

p. 62. "They came . . . gum in my hair." Martin, "Shirley B. Stamps Dies at 59," *The New York Times*, June 4, 2003.

p. 63. I'm glad . . . and others." *Jet,* May 21, 1964.

p. 63. "One winning . . . up there." Greenberg, 167.

Chapter 11

p. 64. "Well before . . . historic case." Greenberg, 179.

p. 65. "Each brief . . . in education." Greenberg, 175.

p. 65. "If I . . . you type it!" Williams, 211.

p. 66. "snide cracks." Williams, 213.

p. 66. "dry run." Greenberg, 178.

p. 66. "We're both . . . your opponent." Williams, 215.

p. 66. "I learned . . . from him." Williams, 214.

p. 66. *Always go* . . . your case." Kluger, 554.

p. 67. "Separate but . . . be overruled." Kluger, 569.

p. 67. "edgy and irritable." Kluger, 564.

p. 67. "It might . . . another place." Kluger, 574; Greenberg, 181.

p. 67. "learned authorities." Kluger, 576.

p. 67. "For some . . . race and color." Kluger, 577.

p. 67. "I know . . . school together." Greenberg, 183.

p. 68. "The strike . . . by outsiders." Kluger, 578.

p. 69. "Separate schools . . . share their schools." Kluger, 582.

p. 69. "kindly feeling." Kluger, 582.

p. 69. "In the heart . . . school system." Greenberg, 185.

p. 69. "I concluded . . . five cases." Greenberg, 185.

p. 69. "I think we've got it won." Kluger, 584.

Chapter 12

p. 70. "All we could do was wait." Greenberg, 189.

p. 70. "not close . . . of problem." Kluger, 593.

p. 71. "Segregation per. . .Fourteenth Amendment." Kluger, 596.

p. 71. "Uphold Seg . . . benefit of both." Kluger, 598 599.

p. 71. "Very simple . . . for education." Kluger, 605606.

p. 72. "putting children together." Kluger, 610.

p. 72. "Agree should . . . as possible." Kluger, 613.

p. 72. "Think wiser . . . equal OK." Kluger, 615.

p. 72. "Segregation in . . . was unconstitutional." Kluger, 617.

p. 72. "We thought . . . quite encouraged." Kluger, 621.

p. 72. "shook us . . . that summer." Kluger, 621-622.

p. 72. "I talked . . . and anxious." Kluger, 623.

p. 72. "I think . . . making history." Kluger, 639.

p. 73. "The man was simply great." Williams, 222.

p. 73. "I never . . . John Franklin." Kluger, 641.

p. 73. "I never . . . those sessions." Kluger, 645.

p. 73. "Everything was torn to pieces." Kluger, 648.

p. 73. "Dollar or . . . the door." Greenberg, 192.

p. 74. "We knew . . . were doing." Interview with author, July 15, 2014.

p. 74. "Mr. Davis . . . case won." Kluger, 650.

p. 74. "in the . . . both races." Kluger, 652.

Chapter 13

p. 75. "There were . . . end segregation." Kluger, 670.

p. 75. "complete legal equality." Kluger, 670.

p. 76. "comingled . . . any more quickly?" Kluger, 675.

p. 76. "That sonofabitch . . . he argues." Greenberg, 203.

p. 77. "He was . . . was arguing." Williams, 224.

p. 77. "Thurgood's rebuttal . . . Constitution stands for." Greenberg, 203-204.

p. 77. "Our Constitution . . . are equal." Greenberg, 205.

p. 77. "under a cloud." Kluger, 680.

p. 77. "I am glad . . . been changed." Kluger, 681.

p. 77. "whether or not . . . shall prevail." Friedman, 6.

p. 78. "I don't . . . to be reached." Kluger, 681-682.

p. 78. "We decided . . . hurry it." Kluger, 686.

Chapter 14

p. 79. "come Hell . . . by '63." Williams, 225.

pp. 79-80. "On freedom's . . . in 1863." Williams, 225.

p. 80. "I have . . . *of Topeka*." Kluger, 705.

p. 80. "firm, clear, and unemotional." Kluger, 705.

p. 80. "In these . . . every to be undone." " Brown v Board of Education." See pp. 115-116.

p. 80. "We conclude . . . inherently unequal." Kluger, 710.

p. 80. "I was . . . was numb." Kluger, 717.

p. 80. "In view . . . Federal Government." Kluger, 711.

p. 81. "We hit the jackpot." Williams, 226.

p. 81. "It is . . . on our side." Williams, 227.

p. 82. "All the kids . . . relate to them." PBS *Newshour*, Transcript, p. 5 of 6.

p. 82. "I feel that . . . child indicated." Millikan, "Negroes to Mark Court Victory Tuesday Night."

p. 82. "The media . . . carries my name." Linda Brown Thompson interview, August 12, 1993.

p. 82. "I'm completely . . . back of segregation." Millikan, "Negroes to Mark Court Victory Tuesday Night."

p. 83. "good news . . . change in Delaware." *Jet*, May 21, 1964.

p. 83. "Barbara was . . . with happiness." Kanefield, 38.

p. 83. "We never . . . historical event." Interview with author.

p. 83. "I wonder . . . changed history." Interview with Eliza Briggs, May 19, 1995.

p. 83. "We always . . . not unanimously." Williams, 229.

p. 83. "I beat . . . who did." Williams, 229.

p. 84. "just sat . . . felt it." Patterson, 71.

p. 84. "It was all . . . would lead." Greenberg, 213.

p. 84. "I don't . . . just begun." Williams, 229.

Chapter 15

p. 85. "was in ashes . . . too surprised."
Interview with author.

p. 85. "We are . . . first magnitude." Pratt, 2.

p. 85. "South Carolina . . . our schools."
Patterson, 78.

pp. 85-86. "I do not . . . won't happen."
Patterson, 78.

p. 86. "This is . . . follow them." Pratt, 3.

p. 86. "Jubilation, optimism . . . important
day." Patterson, 70.

p. 86. "The Supreme . . . Emancipation
Proclamation." Williams, 231.

p. 86. "We assumed . . . in white America?"
Patterson, 70.

p. 87—"I shall use . . . in Virginia."
Pratt, 4.

p. 87. "If they . . . same afternoon." Pratt, 3.

p. 87. "I'm in . . . Advancement of People."
Williams, 231–232.

p. 87. "in no . . . of 1955." Williams, 232.

p. 88. "We were . . . feel intimidated." Camp,
Online Article.

p. 88. "Getting an education . . . greater
opportunities." Milford Live, Nov. 5, 2015.

p. 88. "My mother . . . new clothes." Milford
Live, Nov. 5, 2015.

p. 88. "This was . . . poor black family." Camp
and Kee, 38.

p. 88. "On the first day . . . not friendly."
Milford Live, Nov. 5, 2015.

p. 88. "We stuck . . . eventually integrate."
Camp, Online Article

p. 89. "withdrawal of . . . than whites."
Greenberg, 218.

p. 89. "terrific problems . . . Negro schools."
Kluger, 734.

p. 90. "a death blow to public education."
Kluger, 737.

p. 90. "Texas loves . . . solve it." Kluger,
737-738.

p. 90. "The very people . . . those children."
Kluger, 738.

p. 90. "dumb colored . . . white children."
Williams, 237.

p. 90. "with *all deliberate speed*." Greenberg, 220

p. 90. "The first . . . 'slow speed.'" Williams,
238.

p. 90. "Integration hasn't . . . speed' is."
Williams, 239.

p. 90. "It will not . . . can guarantee." Williams,
238.

Epilogue

p. 91. "Unless our . . . live together." Kluger,
767.

p. 91. "the backlash against our victory."
Greenberg, 215.

p. 92. "Blood will run in the streets." Willias,
263.

p. 92. "During that . . . further proceedings."
Greenberg, 246.

p. 93. "It was . . . the way." Greenberg,
271.

p. 93. "What had . . . efforts achieved?"
Greenberg, 272.

p. 93. "The Brown . . . secondclass citizenship."
PBS *Newshour*, May 12, 2004.

p. 93. "I think . . . facet of life." Interview with
Linda Brown Thompson, August 12, 1993.

p. 94. "Every ten . . . one of us." Interview with
author.

p. 94. "He gave . . . the cheek." Interview with
author.

pp. 94-95. "Today, the hope . . . thrive together." Presidential Proclamation, May 15, 2014.

p. 95. "I had thought . . . hasn't come up yet." Tushnet, Thurgood *Marshall,* 463.

p. 95. "This court . . . giant step backwards." Mr. Justice Marshall, Dissenting, Tushnet, 305.

p. 95. "Bussing became a national issue." Greenberg, 419.

p. 96. " "There are . . . across the nation." Orfield, et. al, "Deepening Segregation in American Public Schools," p. 11

pp. 96-97. "In Tuscaloosa . . . never happened." HannahJones, Radio Broadcast.

p. 97. "Are we . . . is happening." Frankenberg, unpaged.

p. 97. "Schools remain . . . getting worse." Strayss, 2.

p. 97. "more, not . . . integrated education." Frankenberg, *The Civil Rights Project.*

p. 97. "how society has changed." Camp and Kee, 144.

p. 97. "It still . . . racism is wrong." Camp and Kee, 144.

p. 97. "Change doesn't . . . can come true." Camp and Kee, 184 and 186.

p. 97. "Do not . . . to the end." James, 234.

PICTURE CREDITS

Afro-American Newspapers, The: 74, 90

Cobb, Courtesy of Joan Johns: 83, 94

Delaware Public Archives: 54, 55, 57, 63, 84, 86 (top right)

Getty Images/Carl Iwasaki: 14, 20, 22

Getty Images/ Hank Walker/LIFE Picture Collection: 38

Kansas Historical Society: 15, 16, 19 (top), 19 (bottom),

Library of Congress: 10 (top left), 10 (bottom right), 11, 42, 48, 60, 65, 68, 76, 81, 86 (top left), 87, 89, 92, 93 (top), 93 (bottom), 96

Library of Congress/Bradley Smith: x

Library of Congress/Gordon Parks: 29

Library of Congress/Jack Delano: 3, 4

Library of Congress/Lewis Wickes Hine: ii

Library of Congress/Marion Post Wolcott: 98

Lincoln University, Courtesy of Langston Hughes Memorial Library: 8

Mendez family, Courtesy of the: 12

National Archives: 2, 35 (top), 35 (bottom), 36, 43, 44, 45

Supreme Court of the United States, Collection of: 7, 71, 73

South Carolina Department of Archives and History, Courtesy of the: 25 (top), 25 (bottom), 31

Spelman College Archives, Courtesy of the: 34

Stamps, Jr., Courtesy of Phillip E.: 56

Washington Post, Reprinted with permission of the DC Public Library, Star Collection, ©Washington Post: 50 (top), 50 (bottom), 51, 52 (top), 52 (bottom left), 52 (bottom center), 52 (bottom right), 82

ACKNOWLEDGMENTS

Thank you to Cheryl Brown Henderson and the Brown Foundation for guiding me in my research and providing background information, educational resources and contacts. I thank John Watson and Joan Johns Cobb for speaking to me over the phone and sharing their stories. A special thanks to Orlando J. Camp for permitting me to quote him, and to Charles Hammond, President of the Board of the Milford Museum. And I thank June Shagaloff Alexander for generously telling me about assisting Thurgood Marshall at the NAACP Legal Defense and Education Fund.

Many people helped me with the detective work of text and photo research. Without their persistence and dedication I would not have been able to include a great number of vital images and details. So I thank the following:

Phillip E. Stamps, Jr., son of Shirley Barbara Beulah Stamps; Criss Miranda; Sylvia Mendez; Duncan Tonatiuh; Teri Kanefield; Kia Campbell, Duplication Services, Library of Congress; Michele Casto, Special Collections Librarian, Washingtoniana; Julian Hipkins, III, Curriculum Specialist and Missippi Teacher Fellowship Project Director; Debra Hashim and Laura McClure, National Museum of American History; Nancy Sherbert, Curator of Photographs, Kansas State Historical Society; Randy Goss, Delaware Public Archives; Heather Glasby, Archivist, National Archives at Philadelphia; Anne McDonough and Jessica Richardson, The Historical Society of Washington, D.C.; Kassandra A. Ware, Spelman College; Bryan Collars, South Carolina Department of Archives and History; Gretchen Krause and Janet Tramonte, Supreme Court of the United States; Elizabeth Pitt, Lincoln University; Larissa Franklin, Getty Images; Matthew Albright, *The News Journal of Wilmington;* and Gary Emeigh.

As always, I am deeply grateful to my wonderful editor Mary Cash who responded to the idea for this book immediately and worked with me to make it happen. At Holiday House I also thank our superb designer Kerry Martin, our beloved publisher John Briggs, and the whole production, promotion and marketing team.

I will always be indebted to my friend, mentor and agent George Nicholson (1937–2015), who thought it was important to write about the five cases that comprised *Brown v. Board of Education.* And I thank my writer friends at Lunch Bunch and Third Act for their valuable comments and warm support. Last of all, thanks to my son Andrew for patiently helping me solve technical problems, and to my husband Michael for his belief in this book.

INDEX

Page numbers in *italics* refer to illustrations.